D0995600

# ROBERT MUGABE

## Power, Plunder and Tyranny in Zimbabwe

Martin Meredith is the author of

*Nelson Mandela*

*The Past is Another Country*

*The First Dance of Freedom*

*In the Name of Apartheid*

*South Africa's New Era*

*Coming to Terms: South Africa's Search for Truth*

*Africa's Elephant*

He lives near Oxford, England.

# ROBERT MUGABE

Power, Plunder and Tyranny in Zimbabwe

## MARTIN MEREDITH

JONATHAN BALL PUBLISHERS
JOHANNESBURG & CAPE TOWN

Originally published in UK and USA by PublicAffairs™, a Member of Perseus Books LLC

This edition published by
JONATHAN BALL PUBLISHERS (PTY) LTD
PO Box 33977
Jeppestown
2043

ISBN 1 86842 121 X

Martin Meredith has asserted his right to be identified as the author of this Work

.

Text design and reproduction by Mark McGarry, Texas Type and Book Works, USA
Cover and picture sections designed by Michael Barnett, Johannesburg
Cover photograph by AP Photo/Rob Cooper
Reproduction of cover and picture sections by Triple M Design & Advertising, Johannesburg
Printed and bound by CTP Book Printers, Caxton Street, Parow, Cape Town

Our votes must go together with our guns. After all, any vote we shall have, shall have been the product of the gun. The gun which produces the vote should remain its security officer—its guarantor. The people's votes and the people's guns are always inseparable twins.

ROBERT MUGABE, 1976

# CONTENTS

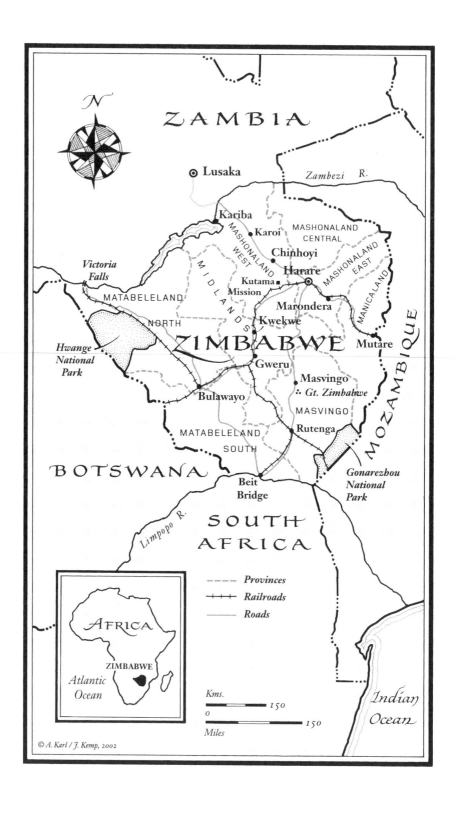

N

ZAMBIA

⊙ Lusaka

*Zambezi R.*

Kariba

● Karoi

MASHONALAND
CENTRAL

MASHONALAND
WEST

*Victoria
Falls*

● Chinhoyi

Harare ⊙

Kutama
Mission

MASHONALAND
EAST

MATABELELAND

MIDLANDS

Marondera

MANICALAND

NORTH

● Kwekwe

ZIMBABWE

Mutare

*Hwange
National
Park*

Gweru

● Masvingo
∴ *Gt. Zimbabwe*

Bulawayo

MASVINGO

MATABELELAND

Rutenga

SOUTH

MOZAMBIQUE

BOTSWANA

Beit
Bridge

*Gonarezhou
National
Park*

*Limpopo R.*

SOUTH
AFRICA

---- *Provinces*

+++ *Railroads*

—— *Roads*

AFRICA

ZIMBABWE

*Atlantic
Ocean*

*Indian
Ocean*

Kms.

0 ▮▮▮ 150

Miles ▮▮▮ 150

© *A. Karl / J. Kemp,* 2002

# [1]

## THE PRIEST AND THE PRESIDENT

FROM THE WINDOW of his book-lined study, Father Dieter Scholz gazed out at the hills surrounding Chishawasha Mission as he reflected on the character and career of Robert Mugabe, the president of Zimbabwe, then in his twenty-second year in power. They had first met at a secret gathering in Salisbury in December 1974 a few days after Mugabe had been released from eleven years' imprisonment during a cease-fire in the guerrilla war against white rule in Rhodesia, as Zimbabwe was then called. Father Scholz, a Jesuit, had been one of the few white priests to support the African nationalist cause. As a member of the Catholic Justice and Peace Commission, he had played a leading role in investigating wartime atrocities by the Rhodesian security forces. Together with a small band of Catholic colleagues, he was regarded by Ian Smith's regime as "an enemy of the state." Smith had seized independence from Britain in 1965, determined to halt the tide of black nationalism sweeping through Africa that had led Britain to hand over its other colonies to African rulers. In the civil war that subsequently broke out in Rhodesia in 1972, Smith acted ruthlessly against his opponents, both black and white. Father Scholz was kept under constant surveillance. With a new cease-fire in place, he and his colleagues had gone to the meeting with Mugabe, in a college building in the city centre, to gain a first-hand account of the negotiations that had led to Mugabe's release. "He was quiet spoken and articulate," recalled Father Scholz. "There was no rancour."

Mugabe told the gathering that during the previous month in Que Que prison he had been in the process of writing a Latin examination for a law degree when an African envoy arrived asking him and other senior members of the banned Zimbabwe African National Union (Zanu) to attend a summit meeting of African leaders in neighbouring Zambia that was intended to pave the way to negotiations for a Rhodesian settlement. He was told the plan was backed by Tanzania's Julius Nyerere, Zambia's Kenneth Kaunda, Mozambique's Samora Machel, and Botswana's Seretse Khama, all of whom had hitherto supported the war effort, allowing guerrillas to use their territories to establish rear bases and supply lines. Also involved in the plan was the South African prime minister, John Vorster, who had provided the Rhodesian security forces with crucial support and who was prepared to lean heavily on Smith to get him to cooperate. As part of the plan, Mugabe was told, the Rhodesian authorities had agreed to his temporary release from prison; a senior white official subsequently visited him to promise that the government would pay for any costs resulting from an interruption to his law examinations.

But Mugabe was hostile to any idea of negotiations. His years of imprisonment had only hardened his resolve to pursue revolution in Rhodesia. Alone among the nationalist leaders, he saw no reason to seek a compromise with Rhodesia's white rulers that would leave the structure of white society largely intact and thwart his hopes of achieving an egalitarian people's state. Whereas other imprisoned nationalists, such as his main rival, Joshua Nkomo, the leader of the Zimbabwe African People's Union (Zapu), were willing to come to terms with Ian Smith, Mugabe regarded armed struggle as an essential part of the process of establishing a new society.

Mugabe's first reaction to the proposal to attend the summit meeting in Lusaka was to turn it down. "We Zanu leaders felt that we could not entertain talks at this stage, that it was too early," he told the Catholic group. Even when the African envoy returned to Que Que prison two days later with a written invitation signed by Nyerere, Kaunda, Machel, and Khama, Mugabe was still reluctant to go. "We were very angry because we thought that the heads of state were selling us out," he explained. Only under duress had he finally agreed to travel to Zambia for a preliminary meeting. "The four heads of state said we could prosecute the war to the end, but if we had a chance to achieve the same aim without bloodshed, we should do so." They also wanted Zanu and Zapu to bury their differences and form a united front for the negotiations. But Mugabe remained recalcitrant. Soon afterwards he returned to his prison cell.

When the summit meeting eventually took place in Lusaka, Zambia, in December 1974, it was a fractious event. The African presidents were infuriated by the continuing divisions between Zanu and Zapu. "Nyerere attacked both Zanu and Zapu," Mugabe reported. "He scolded us and then Kaunda spoke and attacked us still more viciously, calling us treacherous, criminal, selfish and not taking the interests of our people to heart. If we did not comply, he would no longer entertain our military presence in Zambia." Machel, he said, had made similar threats about Mozambique's support.

Faced with those threats, Mugabe ostensibly agreed to form a united front and to accept the plan for negotiation, but he had no intention of adhering to it. "We all had plans for self-preservation," he admitted to the Catholic group.

Upon his release from prison, Mugabe, together with a few trusted colleagues, set about secretly organising recruits for Zanu's guerrilla army, Zanla, based in neighbouring Mozambique. Mugabe was assigned the Salisbury district. He was a frequent visitor to Silveira House, a training centre for black leaders that Jesuit priests had established on land belonging to Chishawasha Mission, fifteen miles east of Salisbury. It was one of the few places in Rhodesia where black politicians and church personnel met regularly to discuss ideas for a new social order. Mugabe's two sisters, Sabina and Bridgette, were employed there to work on development programmes for women. Mugabe was given an office and a telephone there and he lectured on Christianity and socialism.

Silveira House was well known to Smith's security police as a hotbed of dissent and was constantly watched. On days when the presence of the security police was more evident than usual, Father John Dove, a former British army officer who had founded the centre, would discreetly inform the staff, "today we are sailing close to the wind."

In March 1975, shortly after his fiftieth birthday, with the recruitment campaign well under way, Mugabe resolved to head for Mozambique himself. He was ambitious to gain control of Zanu's guerrilla campaign. Before leaving, he went to say farewell to his mother, Bona, at her home near Kutama Mission, west of Salisbury. "I am going to war, whether I shall return or not," he told her. Mugabe's brother, Donato, recalled how their mother wept at the news.

But the security police were already closing in. Returning to Salisbury from Kutama Mission, Mugabe discovered that one of his closest friends, Maurice Nyagumbo, a former prison colleague, had been arrested. Nyagumbo was later sentenced to fifteen years' imprisonment for recruiting Africans to join Zanu in Mozambique, a fate that would also have befallen Mugabe.

Desperate to escape the dragnet, Mugabe sought help from Catholic priests. He made his way to a parish house in Rhodesville, a Salisbury suburb, searching for Father Emmanuel Ribeiro, a prison chaplain who had previously been sympathetic to Zanu detainees, smuggling letters and messages for them. Father Ribeiro agreed to let him hide in the parish house while he worked out an escape route. Father Ribeiro recalled, "I told myself, don't complicate things; do something simple. Get nuns, old nuns."

On the pretext of inviting them for a leisurely drive in the coun-tryside, Father Ribeiro arranged for a group of elderly white Do-minican nuns to cover Mugabe's exit from Salisbury. Unaware of the real purpose of the outing, the nuns were collected from their convent in two cars. One was driven by Father Ribeiro. The other, a yellow Volkswagen, was driven by Sister Mary Aquina, a white uni-versity sociologist and ardent supporter of the African nationalist cause. Sister Mary stopped to collect Mugabe from Rhodesville, while Father Ribeiro picked up another Zanu official, Edgar Tekere, from a separate address. As the cars travelled east from Salisbury, they were stopped at a police roadblock, but the police, seeing the white nuns in the cars and assuming the African passengers were church workers, waved them through.

At a farm in Ruwa, twenty miles from the capital, Mugabe and his white companions parted company. Travelling in Sister Mary's yellow Volkswagen, Mugabe and Tekere set out at midnight for an agricultural cooperative at Nyafaru in the eastern highlands. That night, as friends at Nyafaru prepared to guide them across the bor-der, a look-out spotted the security police approaching. With no time to spare, Mugabe escaped through a back window into the for-est. On April 5, 1975, with the police in close pursuit, he crossed the mountains into Mozambique.

For two years, while Zanu was wracked by internal feuds, Mu-gabe bided his time in exile in Mozambique. But in 1977 he finally succeeded in gaining control of the guerrilla campaign.

In Salisbury, Father Dieter Scholz persevered with the work of the Justice and Peace Commission. Born in Berlin in 1938 and edu-cated by Jesuits, he had been sent to Rhodesia in 1963, speaking lit-tle English and knowing nothing about the country. After studying the chiShona language at Salisbury University, he had been sent to a mission station in northeast Rhodesia, after which he returned to

Salisbury. In 1973, soon after the guerrilla war started, Scholz was told over supper one night by a fellow Jesuit visiting Salisbury from the Zambezi Valley about harsh counter-insurgency measures being used by the Rhodesian security forces. When Scholz informed the Justice and Peace Commission, there was considerable scepticism about the report. Scholz therefore decided to travel to the Zambezi Valley himself to ascertain the facts, bringing back first-hand accounts of security force brutality against civilians. With the support of the Justice and Peace Commission, he began documenting other cases. One volume was published in April 1975; a second volume, dealing with abduction, torture, and murder, was published in 1976. Shortly before a third volume was due to appear in 1977, the police raided the commission's offices and arrested Scholz and other leading members, charging them with offences under the Law and Order (Maintenance) Act, a totalitarian measure used by the government to suppress its opponents. The charges were eventually dropped, but in 1978 Scholz was deported.

By 1979 the guerrilla war had spread to every rural area of Rhodesia. Main roads and railway lines were under frequent attack. White farmers bore the brunt, barricaded at night in fortified homes, living daily with the risks of ambushes and land mines. Despite the death and destruction that white rule had brought, Ian Smith remained obdurate. Only reluctantly did he accept the need for an alliance with the moderate African leader, Bishop Abel Muzorewa, giving way to him as prime minister in 1979; even then, so intent was Smith on showing that whites were effectively still in control that he undermined what little chance of success Muzorewa had of bringing peace.

As the war intensified, Britain launched one last initiative to find a solution, calling for negotiations at a conference to be held in London. Once again Mugabe saw no need to attend. His guerrilla army, Zanla, was planning to embark on a new phase of urban warfare. "We felt we needed yet another thrust, and in the urban areas, in order to bring the fight home to where the whites had their citadels," he recalled. The longer the war lasted, the greater were the prospects for achieving his revolutionary objectives.

Yet again Mugabe faced the wrath of African presidents. Both Samora Machel and Kenneth Kaunda insisted that so damaging were Rhodesian raids on guerrilla bases and supply lines in Mozambique and Zambia that they could no longer afford to support the war effort. Machel, himself a revolutionary leader in the war against Portuguese rule in Mozambique, was blunt: If Mugabe refused to go to London and explore negotiations, then he would close down the liberation war.

Mugabe was furious. "We thought they were selling out," he recalled. "The front-line states said we *had* to negotiate, we *had* to go to this conference. There we were, we thought we were on top of the situation back home, we were moving forward all the time, and why *should* we be denied the ultimate joy of having militarily overthrown the regime here? We felt that would give us a better position. We could then dictate terms."

Mugabe gave in and arrived in London in September 1979, a cold, austere figure who rarely smiled and seemed bent on achieving revolution, whatever the cost. While in exile he had repeatedly insisted on the need for a one-party Marxist state, threatened that Ian Smith and his "criminal gang" would be tried and shot, and warned that white exploiters would not be allowed to keep an acre of land. British officials, although acknowledging his intellectual ability, found him difficult to deal with. "Mugabe could be very unpleasant," recalled Sir Michael Palliser, head of the Foreign Office. "He had a very sharp, sometimes rather aggressive, and unpleasant manner."

For his part, Mugabe distrusted the British as intensely as they distrusted him. "I never trusted the British. Never at all. I did not think they meant well toward us. In the final analysis, I do not think they wanted the liberation movement, and especially the one I led, Zanu, to be the victor." At one point during the Lancaster House conference, Mugabe remarked caustically to British Foreign Secretary Lord Carrington: "It is we who have liberated Rhodesia—you are simply intervening now to take advantage of our victory."

Against all odds, the conference stumbled towards agreement. However, at the final hurdle, Mugabe balked at accepting the cease-fire arrangements and made plans to fly to New York to denounce the Lancaster House proceedings at the United Nations. What stopped him was a direct warning given to him by an envoy from Samora Machel: If he did not sign the agreement, he would be welcomed back to Mozambique and given a beach house where he could write his memoirs, but Mozambique would make no further sacrifices for a cause that could be won at the conference table. In other words, as far as Mozambique was concerned, the war was over.

Mugabe was resentful about the outcome of the conference: "As I signed the document, I was not a happy man at all. I felt we had been cheated to some extent, that we had agreed to a deal which would to some extent rob us of victory we had hoped we would achieve in the field."

The British plan, agreed to at the Lancaster House conference, involved sending out to Rhodesia a British governor, supported by a small team of officials, to hold the ring between an assortment of armies in the hope that the cease-fire would last long enough for elections to be held. It was a perilous venture, likely to explode at the point when the election results were announced.

The man chosen as governor, Christopher Soames, a Tory cabinet minister, had few apparent qualifications for the job. He had never been to Rhodesia or taken any interest in Rhodesian affairs and, as he admitted, his knowledge of the complexities of the conflict was slight. On his arrival in Salisbury on December 12, he spoke of the task ahead in the manner of a Tory grandee: "I want to see the freest, fairest elections possible in this country ... but intimidation is rife, violence is rife.... You must remember this is Africa. This isn't Little Puddleton-on-the-Marsh, and they behave differently here. They think nothing of sticking poles up each other's whatnot, and doing filthy, beastly things to each other. It does happen, I'm afraid. It's a very wild thing, an election."

Mugabe returned to Salisbury on January 27, 1980, nearly five years after his escape into exile, to be given a hero's welcome by one of the largest crowds ever seen in Rhodesia. Banners portraying rocket grenades, land mines, and guns greeted him, and many youths wore tee shirts displaying the Kalashnikov rifle, the election symbol that Zanu wanted but the British had disallowed.

Mugabe himself was unexpectedly conciliatory. In Mozambique, shortly before Mugabe's return to Salisbury, President Samora Machel had intervened to warn Zanu against fighting the election on a revolutionary platform. Machel himself was still struggling to overcome the massive disruption caused in Mozambique at independence in 1975 by the exodus of whites fleeing from the Marxist regime he had instituted. Addressing members of Zanu's central committee, Machel was blunt. "Don't play make-believe Marxist games when you get home," he said. "You will face ruin if you force the whites there into precipitate flight."

Consequently, Mugabe's manifesto was stripped of all reference to Marxism and revolution. It spoke instead of the need to take account of "practical realities" such as the capitalist system, which could not be transformed overnight:

Zanu wishes to give the fullest assurance to the white community, the Asian and coloured [mixed-race] communities that a Zanu government can never in principle or in social or government practice, discriminate against them. Racism, whether practised by whites or blacks, is anathema to the humanitarian philosophy of Zanu. It is as primitive a dogma as tribalism or regionalism. Zimbabwe cannot just be a country of blacks. It is and should remain our country, all of us together.

This message of moderation was largely lost, however, in the uproar over intimidation that erupted at the time of Mugabe's return. All three main parties—Mugabe's Zanu–Patriotic Front, as it was now called, Nkomo's Zapu, and Muzorewa's United African National Congress—were adjudged guilty of using intimidation, but British officials considered Zanu-PF to be the worst culprit by far. In violation of the cease-fire agreement, Mugabe had withheld several thousand guerrillas from holding camps to influence the campaign. The scale of intimidation in eastern Rhodesia, according to British officials, was massive. Neither Nkomo nor Muzorewa supporters had been able to campaign there at all. "The word *intimidation* is mild," roared Nkomo. "People are being terrorised. It is *terror*. There is fear in people's eyes." There were mounting demands for Soames to ban Zanu from participating in the election, as he was empowered to do under the terms of the Lancaster House agreement.

Four days after his return from Mozambique, Mugabe was summoned by Soames for a meeting at Government House, the residence he used in Salisbury. A sprawling bungalow of a type originally designed for Indian earthquake zones, it was surrounded by spacious gardens brimming with roses and exotic flowers that glowed after dark during the warm summer evenings. The ornate rooms, furnished with portraits of Cecil Rhodes, Queen Victoria, and other important personages; the fishponds; and the aviary reflected a gentility that had long since passed. Mugabe arrived in a convoy of battered vehicles crammed with armed bodyguards, who leaped out ahead of him. A British official stepped forward, his arms outstretched. "I'm sorry, but we don't have guns in Government House. Perhaps your people would prefer to wait in the car."

The meeting in the main reception room was icy. As Soames recalled: "I had the same picture that everybody had, that he was something of a Marxist ogre, and that he'd as soon slit your throat as look at you. And that he was 'a bad man.'"

Soames remonstrated with Mugabe over his tactics of intimidation. Mugabe in turn pointed to intimidation by Muzorewa's auxiliaries and the Rhodesian security forces. He saw the meeting merely as part of the British plan to thwart his campaign. "The governor is scared by the prospect of a win by our party," he later said. "He would have preferred Muzorewa to win."

Mugabe's suspicions increased after two assassination attempts were made on his life. The first, on February 6, was clearly the work of amateurs: A grenade thrown at the house he had bought in the former white suburb of Mount Pleasant exploded harmlessly against a garden wall. But the second attempt, on February 10, nearly succeeded. As Mugabe's motorcade was travelling from a political rally in Fort Victoria to the airport there, a massive bomb placed in a culvert on the roadside exploded only seconds after Mugabe's car passed over. Mugabe was shaken but not hurt. In a memorandum Mugabe gave Soames two days later, he blamed the security forces for the assassination attempt and listed numerous examples of the ways in which, he claimed, the British authorities, acting in collusion with the Rhodesian administration, were trying to destroy his party. Their exchanges became increasingly acrimonious.

As the election approached, Soames was required to decide whether to take action against Zanu, either by banning it from areas directly affected by intimidation or disqualifying it altogether. The Rhodesian security forces, Muzorewa, and Nkomo all urged him to disqualify Zanu; even his closest advisers were in favour of a ban. But Soames eventually concluded that Mugabe was likely to win the election by such an overwhelming margin that imposing a partial ban would make little difference to the outcome and would wreck whatever chances there were of working with Mugabe to achieve an orderly transition. The risk was that the Rhodesian security forces, furious at the prospect of Mugabe winning, might stage a coup.

The day before polling began on February 27, Soames called Mugabe to Government House, deciding that what was needed was a private meeting alone in his study to try to overcome the distrust with which he and Mugabe had viewed one another. There, Soames informed Mugabe that he would not be using his powers to ban polling or disenfranchise voters in any part of the country. "I think it's in the best interests of Rhodesia that all parties start this election," he said.

Mugabe was relieved but outwardly showed little reaction. Soames then steered the conversation towards the post-election period, asking how Mugabe saw the future. Mugabe paused. There would be no radical change, no hounding of the whites, no nationalisation, he said. He was deeply conscious of the shortcomings of his own team, their lack of political, administrative, and economic experience and skills. Independence should not come too quickly after the election. "I would like you to stay on for as long as possible," he told Soames. They parted amicably.

There remained the possibility of a coup. With Soames's encouragement, Mugabe invited General Peter Walls, the Rhodesian armed forces commander, to a private meeting later that night at his new Mount Pleasant home. There Mugabe asked him to stay on as armed forces commander if he won the election. Walls recalled: "I said to him, but how can I as an avowed anti-Marxist work for a person like you? He gave me a lecture on how the principles of Karl Marx were the same as Jesus Christ." Unknown to Mugabe, Walls sent a message to the British prime minister, Margaret Thatcher, asking her to abrogate the elections because of intimidation.

Walls made one further attempt to block the election. On March 2, while the counting of the votes was still under way, he summoned two of Soames's senior officials to a tense meeting at security force headquarters. "We asked that the elections be set aside, declared not free and fair," he recalled. Other officers raged at what they considered to be British perfidy. The two officials faced such a barrage of abuse that they feared a coup was imminent. Robin Renwick, Soames's political adviser, recalled: "We said that we had promised a free and fair election—there has been an election which, broadly speaking, was free and fair, and we are going to help the government which emerged from it in every way we can."

When the election results were announced on the morning of March 4, Mugabe's victory was so overwhelming that arguments over the effect of intimidation became largely irrelevant. With 63 percent of the national vote, Zanu gained fifty-seven of the eighty black seats in parliament. More than anything else, it was a vote for peace. As most blacks well knew, any other result would almost certainly have led to a resumption of war.

The shock for the whites was all the more profound because they had been convinced, until the last minute, that either Muzorewa would win or at least an anti-Mugabe coalition would be possible. A black Marxist government had been their greatest dread all along; yet suddenly, so it seemed, one was upon them. Within hours, civil service resignations poured in; husbands phoned wives telling them to pack a bag and leave for South Africa; children had even been sent to school that morning carrying bags packed for flight in case rumours about the election results were true.

Less than twelve hours later, the panic began to subside. That evening Mugabe appeared on television; far from being the Marxist ogre the whites feared, he impressed them as a model of moderation. He called for stability, national unity, and law and order; promised that civil service pensions would be guaranteed; and pledged that private property would be protected. "There is no intention on our part to use our majority to victimise the minority. We will ensure there is a place for everyone in this country.... Let us deepen our sense of belonging and engender a common interest that knows no race, colour or creed."

To most whites, who had never seen him before, Mugabe ap-

peared articulate, thoughtful, and conciliatory. What further molli-
fied them was his decision to retain General Walls as overall commander of the security forces. The emphasis that Mugabe placed on
his intention to build on existing institutions of state and to transform the capitalist system gradually, and his assurances that there
would be no nationalisation of farms, mines, or industry, were not
entirely trusted, but in view of what had been expected, the future
of the whites seemed not as bleak as it had on the morning of
March 4. Even Ian Smith, who only a few weeks before had denounced Mugabe as "the apostle of Satan," now found him "sober
and responsible."

In the aftermath of the election, Mugabe turned regularly to
Soames for help and advice, calling on him every day at Government House. At their first meeting, shortly after the election results
had been announced, Mugabe arrived composed and calm but
daunted by the magnitude of the task he faced, as Soames's private
secretary, Jim Buckley, recalled: "He said, 'I have no experience of
running a country and neither has any of my people. None of us has
run anything and so we need your help.'" At a subsequent meeting,
Mugabe asked Soames to stay on as governor for an extended period. "Soames said, 'I have a job back in the UK, but we could
stretch it to the end of the month.' Mugabe said, 'No, No, I am talking about maybe one, two or three years.' Soames said, 'sorry, but
that's totally out of the question.'"

Nevertheless, the help that Soames gave Mugabe in the weeks
before Independence Day on April 18 was crucial in ensuring an orderly transition. For his part, Mugabe was profusely thankful.
Soames, remarked Mugabe, was "so good a friend."

"I must admit that I was one of those who originally never
trusted him. And yet I ended up not only implicitly trusting him but
also fondly loving him as well," he added.

In the hours before midnight on April 17, 1980, political leaders
and dignitaries from around the world gathered in a football stadium

in Salisbury to witness the birth of Zimbabwe. Mugabe marked the
occasion with a speech pledging reconciliation: "If yesterday I
fought you as an enemy, today you have become a friend and ally
with the same national interest, loyalty, rights and duties as myself. If
yesterday you hated me, you cannot avoid the love that binds you to
me and me to you." He said he would "draw a line through the past"
to achieve reconciliation. "The wrongs of the past must now stand
forgiven and forgotten. If ever we look to the past, let us do so for
the lesson the past has taught us, namely that oppression and racism
are inequalities that must never find scope in our political and social
system. It could never be a correct justification that because the
whites oppressed us yesterday when they had power, the blacks must
oppress them today because they have power. An evil remains an evil
whether practised by white against black or black against white." He
called for a new vision and a new spirit.

Zimbabwe, it seemed, was on the threshold of an era of great
promise, born out of civil war but now bursting with new ambition.
Mugabe himself was widely acclaimed a hero: the revolutionary
leader who had embraced the cause of reconciliation and who now
sought a pragmatic way forward. Western governments lined up
with offers of aid. Amid the jubilation, President Nyerere of Tanzania advised Mugabe: "You have inherited a jewel. Keep it that way."


Father Dieter Scholz returned to Zimbabwe in 1990 to work at
Mary Mount Mission in a remote rural parish in Rushinga district,
close to the border with Mozambique. The area had suffered heavily during the war. Father Scholz had first worked there as a missionary in the early 1960s and again in the early 1970s, just before
the war began. He was shocked by what he found on his return:

> The price this remote district paid for the liberation of Zimbabwe
> was staggering. Four out of every five young men I had taught

twenty years earlier and who had joined the struggle, had not come back and no one knew where they had fallen and been buried. A whole generation seemed to be missing in Rushinga.

Equally shocking was the indifference of Mugabe's government to the area's plight. During the war the Rhodesian security forces had destroyed virtually all cattle, deliberately infecting them with anthrax as a communal punishment of the local population for supporting the guerrillas and to deny the guerrillas food. Ten years after independence, there was not a single head of cattle in the whole of eastern Rushinga. "Despite many promises, by 1990 the government had still not given the people a single cow or ox," Scholz recalled. Peasants tried to plough their fields with small home-made hoes, harvesting barely enough to survive.

> Each year, during the rains, we found the skeletons of Zanla fighters—sometimes in the bush, often in the fields and, on one occasion, crouching in a cave—but it was not until the 1990s that a cemetery was set up near Rushinga to give them a decent burial.
>
> Party officials came and went. They promised to match every coffin which the Mission would donate with one of their own. With funds from abroad we paid skilled wood workers to make coffins. They were extremely well crafted. But when the time of the solemn re-burial came, only half the bodies could be laid to rest because the coffins promised by the party had not materialised.

In the capital, renamed Harare, the new black elite scrambled for property, farms, and businesses. Mugabe joined the fray, but his real obsession was not with personal wealth but with power. Year by year, he acquired ever greater power, ruling the country through a vast system of patronage, favouring loyal aides and cronies with government positions and contracts and ignoring the spreading blight of corruption. "I am rich because I belong to Zanu-PF," boasted one of Mugabe's protégés, Phillip Chiyangwa, a millionaire businessman. "If you want to be rich you must join Zanu-PF." One by one, state corporations and funding organisations were plundered. In the most notorious case, a state fund set up to provide compensation for war victims was looted so thoroughly by Mugabe's colleagues that nothing was left for genuine war victims. An official inquiry into the scandal named prominent politicians, including cabinet ministers, among the culprits, but no action was ever taken against them. It was as if Mugabe and his inner circle had come to regard Zimbabwe as the spoils of war, for their own use.

Ordinary people meanwhile suffered the brunt of government mismanagement. By 2000, Zimbabweans were generally worse off than they had been at independence: average wages were lower, unemployment had trebled, public services were crumbling, and life expectancy was falling.

As opposition to his rule mounted, Mugabe struck back with increasing ruthlessness, determined to stay in power whatever the cost, just as Ian Smith had done. "I do not want to be overthrown and I will try to overthrow those who want to overthrow me," he declared at a state banquet in 2000. Reverting to the role of guerrilla leader, he claimed his "revolution" was under attack from his old enemies: the whites, the British, and the West. It was the whites who were responsible for Zimbabwe's economic plight, he told a party congress. "They are trying to sabotage the economy in their fight against the government." He urged supporters "to strike fear in the hearts of the white man, our real enemy."

In an attempt to bolster his popularity, Mugabe sent gangs of party activists—"war veterans," as they were called—to rural areas to seize control of hundreds of white-owned farms for redistribution to peasant farmers. When the courts ruled the land seizures were illegal, Mugabe turned to vilifying judges: "No judicial decision will stand in our way," he declared. Anyone who opposed him he threatened with reprisals. A Catholic archbishop who criticised his conduct of government received death threats from the secret police. All black opponents he denounced as mere dupes of the whites, and he gave "war veterans" licence to attack and terrorise opposition supporters at will. The police were instructed not to intervene and often stood by watching violence and beatings take place. The campaign of intimidation by "war veterans" spread to factories, businesses, and offices; even foreign embassies and aid agencies whom Mugabe accused of supporting the opposition were caught up in the mayhem.

"This is no longer a free country," protested the Conference of Religious Superiors of the Catholic Church after a meeting in March 2001. "People now live in abject fear of violence, crime and threats. The rule of law is no longer respected; terror and intimidation go unpunished."

In his study at Chishawasha Mission, Father Scholz turned his attention to compiling the annual report for 2001 for Silveira House, the training centre near Harare that he now headed. He decided not to write the usual account of workshops and seminars but to address more fundamental issues. Referring to President Nyerere's remark to Mugabe at the independence celebrations, he chose as the title "Whatever Happened to the Jewel?"

Scholz recalled the time when Zimbabwe offered great hope for the future, when it was fêted by the international community and lavished with promises of aid. And he asked: "Whatever happened, in just twenty years, to make this country and its extraordinarily resourceful and courageous people the pariah of the same international community—despised, ridiculed and isolated?"

# [2]

# THE MAKING OF A REVOLUTIONARY

LIKE MANY OTHER African independence leaders, such as Tanzania's Julius Nyerere and Zambia's Kenneth Kaunda, Robert Mugabe was a product of the missionary system. From early childhood, his mentor had been the Catholic Church. He was born on February 21, 1924, in the "Christian village" at Kutama Mission in the Zvimba district, west of Salisbury, established by Jesuit Fathers for Africans who had been baptised. Both his parents were mission trained: His father was a carpenter; his mother, Bona, was a devout and pious woman who taught the catechism and the Bible. His Jesuit teachers were strict disciplinarians, and Mugabe himself developed a belief in the need for self-discipline that was almost puritanical in its intensity. "I was brought up by the Jesuits and I'm most grateful," he recalled. "I benefited from their teaching enormously." At one stage, his mother thought he might become a priest.

Catholic missionaries had set up their first "Christian village" at Chishawasha Mission on land given to them by Cecil Rhodes's private commercial enterprise, the British South Africa Company, which had declared the occupation of Mashonaland in 1890 in the name of Queen Victoria. The land was a reward for the role the Jesuits had played in accompanying the Pioneer Column of white settlers that Rhodes had sent across the Limpopo River to search for gold and extend the realms of the British Empire. Like all the land that Rhodes handed out to white settlers, the land at Chishawasha—some 12,000 acres—was acquired by dispossessing the local population. When the Shona rebellion against white rule broke out in 1896, only six years after the Union Jack had been hoisted near a hill called Harare, the mission station at Chishawasha, along with hundreds of white farms, was engulfed in the violence.

Once the rebellion had been suppressed, the Jesuits returned to Chishawasha, establishing a self-sufficient Christian farming community there. They built a school, a clinic, workshops, and a compound for African Christian families. Jesuits taught skilled trades such as carpentry, stonemasonry, shoemaking, and horticulture, while Dominican nuns concentrated on domestic science and child care. Chishawasha soon became a model for other mission stations that the Catholic Church established throughout Rhodesia.

Kutama Mission, an offshoot of Chishawasha, achieved a particular distinction. When Mugabe was seven years old, an Irish Jesuit, Father Jerome O'Hea, took charge as the new supervisor. A strong believer in education as the key to emancipation, he devoted his efforts and much of his personal fortune to founding a teacher training school and a hospital. Kutama's reputation soon spread far afield, attracting students from across Rhodesia and from neighbouring countries. One of them, Lawrence Vambe, a journalist, recalled his time there in the early 1930s in his memoirs: "Here was young Africa, full of hope and zeal, brought together under the umbrella of this institution, where we were all trying to gain a deeper insight into the white world, as well as break away from our own tribal chains."

As a child, Mugabe was secretive and solitary. He spent much time on his own, preferring to read rather than participate in sports or other school activities. "His only friends were books," his brother, Donato, recalled. He was remembered in particular for his serious demeanour—what Father O'Hea later described as "unusual gravitas." Because of his aptitude for learning, he was invariably the youngest boy in his class. "I suppose the fact that he was younger and smaller may have kept him a little apart from everyone," recalled a school friend, David Garwe. "I don't remember him taking part in sport or school plays. He always seemed to enjoy his own company."

At the age of ten Mugabe was struck by a family calamity. His father, Gabriel, left Kutama to find employment in Bulawayo but never returned, deserting his wife and six children for another woman, with whom he had three children. Mugabe, his brothers, and his sisters were consequently brought up in straitened circumstances by his mother and grandparents. "Mugabe has never forgiven him for that," recalled a family cousin, James Chikerema, in an interview in 2000. In later years Mugabe lavished fulsome praise on his mother but never once mentioned his father. Even after he had been in power for twenty years, so little was known about his father and the circumstances in which he abandoned his young family that the local press still speculated about who he really was, whether he was perhaps a foreigner.

The bright youngster soon came to the attention of Father O'Hea. After he had completed six grades of elementary education, Father O'Hea offered Mugabe a course in his teacher training school, helping him pay his tuition fees with his own funds. "I would have kept him for nothing because of his influence over the other boys. Before long he was teaching his classmates how to teach."

As well as instructing Mugabe on the catechism and Cartesian logic, Father O'Hea gave him a feel for Irish legend and revolution, describing the struggle the Irish had sustained to attain independence from Britain. Shortly before his death in 1970, Father O'Hea recalled how Mugabe possessed what he called "an exceptional mind and an exceptional heart." Mugabe in turn acknowledged the formative influence of Father O'Hea. During the Lancaster House conference in London in 1979, he told a priest with whom he was friendly that one day he would like to pray at O'Hea's grave.

Outside the mission system, Mugabe faced the reality of white supremacy. "We were brought up in a society which actually worshipped the white man as a kind of god," Mugabe recalled in an interview after he had become prime minister.

> He was infallible. He was the ruler to be obeyed. Whoever was white therefore not only had the power but also the privilege of demanding respect from every black. And so we feared the white man.
>
> After the defeat of the blacks in 1897, our parents and grandparents accepted rule by the white man as something unavoidable. There was no way we could get rid of the white man. He was power. He had guns. He had subdued everybody through the security forces. And therefore all we could do was to seek from him the removal of our grievances. If we could get some form of justice within the system, that was all that people sought to be achieved. And we accepted this as youngsters.

Mugabe left Kutama in 1945 with a teaching diploma to take up a series of teaching posts, moving restlessly from one school to the next but remaining dedicated to his work and using every moment of his spare time to study. In 1949 he won a scholarship to Fort Hare University College in South Africa, the elite black institution where Nelson Mandela had studied ten years before, finding himself for the first time in a political hothouse. It was at Fort Hare that Mugabe was introduced to Marxist ideas, joining in discussions with South African communists and reading Marxist literature. But the most important influence on him at the time, he said, was Mahatma Gandhi, whose passive resistance campaign against British rule in India had fired the imagination of many young African nationalists. "This gave me personally a new kind of vision, a new philosophy, that if Africans were united in the same way as the Indians were, even if they resorted to a non-violent struggle, they would eventually emerge victorious."

By the time that Mugabe returned to Southern Rhodesia in 1952, armed with a degree, his views had changed radically. "I was completely hostile to the system," he said, adding, "but of course I came back to teach within it." Although more politically aware, he still preferred to continue his studies rather than engage in political activity, and he enrolled for a degree by correspondence from the University of South Africa. He ordered copies of *Das Kapital* and other Marxist tracts from a London mail order firm but showed no sign of political commitment.

Mugabe often dominated discussion groups. "He had this wide range of interests," recalled Guy Clutton-Brock, a white liberal who regularly held meetings with African teachers. "He could talk about Elvis Presley or Bing Crosby as easily as politics."

But while Mugabe always impressed others with the broad range of his knowledge, he remained an aloof and austere figure. Clutton-Brock admitted finding him "a bit of a cold fish at times." He neither drank nor smoked. Smoking, Mugabe once said, did not "make any sense" to him; as for drink, "What really does one enjoy by getting drunk and allowing moments when one is not in control of oneself?" To his political friends in the 1950s he remained something of an enigma: a nationalist in heart and mind but one who kept his distance.

In 1955 Mugabe moved to Northern Rhodesia (now Zambia) to take up a post at a teacher training college in Lusaka. He took little interest in politics there, spending his spare time gaining a third degree by correspondence from London University. In 1958 he moved on again, this time to a job at the Takoradi Teacher Training College in Ghana.

Ghana at that time was a place of high excitement. As the first

black African colony to gain independence, it abounded with opti-
mism and ambition. Its new leader, Kwame Nkrumah, having challenged the might of British rule in Africa, saw himself as a
revolutionary leader destined to play an even greater role in Africa.
At home he wanted to transform Ghana into an industrial power, a
centre of learning, a model socialist society that other states would
want to emulate. He dreamed of making Africa a giant in economic,
political, and military terms, as united and powerful as the United
States and the Soviet Union, with himself as leader. He was determined in particular to turn Ghana into a launching pad for African
liberation, providing a base from which nationalist leaders from
colonial Africa could draw support and encouragement.

Mugabe revelled in this environment, soaking up the ambition
and the rhetoric around him. Africans were everywhere gaining
swift advancement, not only in government but in the civil service,
in commerce and industry, and in schools. "I went as an adventur-
ist," he recalled. "I wanted to see what it would be like in an independent African state. Once there I began to develop definite ideas.
You could say that it was there I accepted the general principles of
Marxism."

While teaching in Takoradi Mugabe became enamoured of a fellow teacher, Sally Heyfron, the daughter of an agricultural teacher
at the same college. Their courtship was not especially romantic:
Sally recalled, twenty years later, that they had never been to see a
movie together. Politics were their main source of enjoyment. "He
became my inspiration," said Sally. "He politicised me." They decided to marry but were still unsure whether to live in Ghana or
Rhodesia.


In Rhodesia the political tempo had changed. In 1957 a new nationalist organisation, the African National Congress (ANC), had been
launched. To avoid alarming the white population, it set out to pro-

ject a moderate image. The central theme of its platform was non-racialism and economic progress; it suggested the abolition of discriminatory laws, reform of land allocation, and an extension of the franchise. Although the franchise was non-racial, the qualifications for a vote, based on income, were so high that at the time, of an electorate of 52,000, only 560 were Africans.

The ANC's leader, Joshua Nkomo, was chosen because of his moderate credentials. Born in 1917, the son of a relatively prosperous teacher and lay preacher who worked for the London Missionary Society in the Semokwe reserve, south of Bulawayo, he had proved a skilful negotiator as a railway union official and was known for his work in multiracial and church circles; on Sundays he was a lay preacher in the British Methodist Church.

Within a short time the ANC succeeded in establishing a mass movement both in urban and rural areas. Poverty and frustration in the towns and overcrowding in rural areas had produced a groundswell of discontent. There was particular resentment in rural areas over the government's land policies: Over a period of thirty years, more than half a million Africans had been uprooted from their homes on land designated to be "white" areas.

The Rhodesian government responded ruthlessly to the nationalist challenge. Although there was no open disorder in Rhodesia at the time, the ANC was banned in February 1959 on the grounds that the nationalists were inciting the black population to defy the law and ridicule government authority. More than 500 Africans were arrested and 300 detained.

Nkomo escaped the dragnet. In December 1958 he had left Rhodesia to attend a conference on African liberation organised by Kwame Nkrumah in Accra and had since developed a fondness for foreign travel. When the ANC was banned, he was in Cairo. He travelled to London, established a base there, and did not go back to Rhodesia until November 1960.

Undaunted by government repression, in January 1960 the nationalists in Rhodesia launched a new organisation, the National Democratic Party (NDP), putting forward a more radical platform. They demanded not simply the redress of grievances over land and discrimination but political power as well. One of the NDP's founding fathers, Leopold Takawira, declared: "We are no longer asking Europeans to rule us well. We now want to rule ourselves." Convinced that the key to their advancement lay with Britain, the nationalists spent much of their energy trying to persuade the British government to intervene to curb the white politicians in Salisbury, by force if necessary. But Britain, which had granted Rhodesia self-governing status under white control in 1923, showed no inclination to get involved.

In May 1960 Mugabe returned to Rhodesia on long leave, bringing Sally to introduce her to his mother and family before they married. He fully intended to go back to Ghana to complete his four-year teaching contract once his holiday was over, but he soon found himself caught up in the drama of the times. Nationalist friends, notably Leopold Takawira, a Catholic teacher whom he had known from his student days at Kutama Mission, urged him to stay and join the cause. Mugabe was still considering what to do when, on July 19, police arrested three prominent NDP officials, including Takawira, after a dawn search of their houses and the party's offices, charging them under sections of the Unlawful Organisations Act. That night Mugabe joined a crowd of about 7,000 Africans that set out from the black suburb of Highfield to march the eight miles into Salisbury, intending to protest outside the prime minister's office. At Stodart Hall in Harare township they were stopped by police in full riot gear.

By midday the next day the crowd had swelled to 40,000. A makeshift platform was built for speakers to address the crowd, and Mugabe was among those asked to speak. Introduced as a distinguished scholar who had travelled in Africa and who possessed three university degrees, he began to talk about his vision for the future of "Zimbabwe," the name the nationalist movement used for Rhodesia, adopted from the site of impressive stone ruins near Masvingo that five centuries before had been the political and religious capital of a black monarchy. When he finished, the crowd gave him a rousing round of applause.

The government's response to the protest eventually was to order the police to break it up. It followed with a piece of legislation, the Law and Order (Maintenance) Act, designed to deal with any future African opposition. The Act's provisions were so sweeping that, if fully enforced, they would have obliterated any notion of liberty and individual rights. They enabled the government to curb freedom of speech, movement, privacy, assembly, and association, and to arrest and detain anyone without trial. The legislation so appalled the chief justice, Sir Robert Tredgold, that he resigned. "This bill outrages every basic right," he said. "If passed into law, it will remove the last vestige of doubt about whether Rhodesia is a police state."

The March of the 7,000, as it became known, and the events that followed, propelled Mugabe into the nationalist fray. He resigned from his teaching post in Ghana and became a full-time activist. At the inaugural NDP congress in October 1960 he was elected publicity secretary and developed a fine line in angry rhetoric.

He wrote to Sally, who had returned to Ghana, asking her to join him in Rhodesia and to marry him there. They were married in a Catholic ceremony in Salisbury in February 1961, knowing full well how difficult their married life was likely to be. "When I went to Zimbabwe," Sally recalled. "I didn't think I was just going to sit on the fence. I knew when I went that I would be involved." Sally quickly won the admiration of Mugabe's friends for her vivacious nature. "She was always at the centre of laughter," a friend recalled.

In an attempt to resolve Rhodesia's constitutional future, the British government convened a conference in Salisbury in 1961, which NDP officials were invited to attend. It was the most valuable opportunity the nationalists were given in the 1960s to make their mark. The NDP team was led by Joshua Nkomo, who had been chosen as NDP president on his return to Rhodesia a few months before.

Nkomo's performance was indecisive and inept. He assumed that any agreement at the conference would assist the nationalist cause and lead towards African rule, as other constitutional conferences the British had arranged for their African colonies had done. But the objectives of the British and Rhodesian governments were discernibly different. The principal aim of the Rhodesians was to acquire virtual autonomy under white minority rule. The British government was anxious to disengage from Rhodesia and was prepared to give Rhodesians the degree of autonomy they wanted provided African advancement was recognisably established.

To Mugabe's fury, Nkomo accepted a deal that gave the nationalists fifteen out of sixty-five parliamentary seats based on a complex franchise that would have delayed majority rule for several decades. No sooner were the results known than a storm of protest broke out in the NDP. After ten days, Nkomo was obliged to repudiate the deal. But by then it was too late. If he had rejected the proposals in negotiations, the British government would almost certainly have been forced to convene another conference. As it was, the new constitution became law in 1962.

The nationalists soon fell into disarray. Hoping that the British government would intervene to support new demands, particularly if it appeared that foreign investment was endangered, they refused to participate in any activity related to the new constitution and resorted to reckless violence to prevent black voters from registering for the 1962 elections. African homes, schools, beer halls, and shops were looted and burned; gangs of youths roamed the African suburbs seeking anyone who was identified with the government or was not a party member.

Mugabe threatened to widen the action. "Europeans must realise that unless the legitimate demands of African nationalism are recognised, then racial conflict is inevitable," he declared. At political rallies he spoke of the need for self-sacrifice, telling crowds to take off their socks and shoes as a sign they were willing to reject European civilisation. "Today you have removed your shoes. Tomorrow you may be called upon to destroy them altogether, or to perform other acts of self-denial," he told an NDP meeting in Highfield in December 1961. "If European-owned industries are used to buy guns which are aimed against us, we must withdraw our labour and our custom, and destroy those industries."

It was the NDP's last rally. Six days later the government banned the party. Within days the nationalists responded by launching a new organisation, the Zimbabwe African People's Union (Zapu), with identical aims and tactics. The violence increased. White targets were now included; forests and crops were burned, cattle maimed, sabotage attempts made on railway lines, and attacks carried out on schools and churches.

During the turmoil, Nkomo indulged his manifest fondness for foreign travel, touring the world seeking international support, leaving the nationalist movement bereft of effective leadership. He appeared to have no coherent plan other than to rely on international opinion to force Britain to intervene and implement majority rule. His prolonged absences, his reluctance to face the issues at home, and his indecisiveness all caused mounting dissatisfaction amongst party officials, especially intellectuals like Mugabe. Confrontation in Rhodesia was what was needed, they argued, not pseudo-diplomacy.

Zapu survived for no more than nine months before it was banned. In September 1962 Mugabe and other officials were arrested and restricted to their home districts for three months. An English academic, Claire Palley, who met him in restriction, found him an impressive figure. "The quality most apparent was his intellectual rigour," she recalled. "He had this ability to listen to argument, then dissect it, take it to bits."

Nkomo at first escaped arrest. He was out of the country at the time of the ban, visiting Lusaka on the final stage of a return journey to Salisbury. Beset by indecision, unsure whether he should continue to Rhodesia or remain outside to direct the party's external affairs, he went into hiding, drove off in secret to Dar es Salaam, and eventually had to be persuaded by Julius Nyerere, the new leader of Tanganyika (later part of Tanzania) to suffer the consequences back home. On his return, he was restricted to a village in the Semokwe reserve, south of Bulawayo.

The threat that African ferment inside Rhodesia posed to white rule produced a growing white backlash. In December 1962 a new right-wing party, the Rhodesian Front, with the strong support of white farmers worried about their right to land, won the election. Once in power, the Rhodesian Front became obsessed with the need for independence from Britain. They also moved swiftly to tighten up security laws, introducing tough amendments to the Law and Order (Maintenance) Act, including a mandatory death sentence for sabotage.

Amongst the nationalists there was much talk of violence. After his restriction order was lifted, Mugabe returned to Salisbury, to his small house in Highfield, where colleagues gathered to discuss what strategy to adopt. Three parties had been banned, and each time the nationalists had lost hard-won property, vehicles, and funds. "The question was, should we continue as before with a political struggle, campaigning and demonstrations, or were we now going to embark on a programme that would lead to an armed struggle, the training of our people?" Mugabe recalled. "And we agreed that we had to train people."

Nkomo, however, had different ideas. While under restriction he had become convinced that the only effective way to continue the nationalist campaign was for Zapu's executive to leave the country and set up a government-in-exile. If the Rhodesian Front seized independence, then the nationalists would be able to claim international recognition. He sent messages to members of the national executive asking them to meet him in the Semokwe reserve. For many of them, including Mugabe, this meant breaking the conditions of their restriction and risking imprisonment. When they heard what Nkomo was proposing, they turned the idea down flat.

Upon his release from restriction in January 1963, Nkomo resumed his travels to lobby foreign governments and returned to Rhodesia at the end of March with the news that African leaders, like Nyerere, thought it advisable for the entire Zapu executive to leave the country and establish a base in Dar es Salaam.

For Mugabe in particular this posed a dilemma. Shortly beforehand he had been charged with subversion after making a speech in Salisbury in which he accused the "gangster" government of "planning murder." The trial date had been set. Leaving Rhodesia meant breaking bail.

Moreover, Sally was also entangled with the law. She too had been charged with making a subversive statement in a speech in which she had attacked Britain for abandoning the blacks in Rhodesia. "The Queen can go to hell," she had declared. For this offence she had already been sentenced to two years' imprisonment, fifteen months of which had been suspended. She was now out on bail pending an appeal. An additional concern was that she was pregnant. The previous year the Mugabes had lost their first child at birth. This second pregnancy was also proving difficult. However, on hearing that Nyerere supported the idea, the Mugabes were reluctantly persuaded that they should leave.

When members of the Zapu executive gathered in Dar es Salaam in April, they discovered that neither Nyerere nor any other African leader approved the idea of a government-in-exile. Indeed, Nyerere insisted that resistance inside Rhodesia was the only answer. When Nkomo attended a summit meeting of African leaders in May seeking funds to maintain the party leadership in exile, he was rebuffed. Nkomo's foreign expertise, which at one time seemed such a valuable asset, no longer seemed to count for much. In Rhodesia all organised activity had come to a halt. Neither at home nor abroad was Zapu making any headway. Nkomo's critics decided a change of leadership was imperative.

Mugabe was foremost among these critics. But whereas Nkomo was able to return to Rhodesia freely, Mugabe found himself stranded in Dar es Salaam with a pregnant wife, facing not only a trial back home for subversion but new charges for breaking his bail. He stayed on in Dar es Salaam for a few months more. In August Sally gave birth to a son, whom they named Nhamodzenyika, a Shona word meaning "suffering country." But Mugabe knew that eventually he would have to return home. He insisted, however, that Sally should not face a prison sentence and should instead take the child to Ghana, to her parents.

In Salisbury Mugabe's colleagues launched the Zimbabwe African National Union (Zanu), choosing Ndabaningi Sithole, a mission-educated teacher and church minister, as leader. Mugabe was elected secretary-general in absentia. The announcement was made on August 8 in the tiny home in Highfield of Enos Nkala, a volatile Ndebele politician who harboured an abiding hatred for Nkomo. Addressing the press, Nkala declared: "Now I am going to see to it that Joshua Nkomo is crushed." Ten days later Nkomo responded by launching another new party, the People's Caretaker Council. In effect, it represented the loyal contingent of Zapu and continued to be known as Zapu.

The differences between the two groups were at first negligible. Both advocated the same goal of majority rule, continued to seek external support and to lobby the British government, established external bases in Africa to coordinate their foreign activities, and recruited members for guerrilla training outside the country. Initially tribal loyalties were not directly affected. Although most of the Ndebele and Kalanga stood by Nkomo, both groups drew supporters from the same Shona areas. Nkomo's strongest support came from Salisbury and Bulawayo, the capital of Matabeleland; Zanu's from the south, east, and Midlands. What difference there was lay largely in rhetoric.

As each group tried to assert itself, however, the rivalry developed into uncontrolled violence. Gang warfare, petrol bombing, arson, stoning, and assaults became commonplace. Little attention was paid either to whites or to the causes the nationalists were ostensibly serving.

The spectacle of nationalist strife caused disenchantment among nationalist sympathisers abroad, provided evidence for Rhodesian whites who maintained that black rule would inevitably end in turmoil, and eventually gave the government a sufficient pretext for crushing the nationalist movement in the name of law and order. In time, the split assumed tribal and ideological dimensions that were never overcome.

Amid the mayhem, Mugabe returned to Rhodesia in December 1963. He was arrested on arrival and remanded in custody. At his trial he refused to retract any of the subversive statements he was accused of making, and in March 1964 he was sentenced to twenty-one months' imprisonment.

Other nationalist leaders were placed in restriction. In April Nkomo was sent to a camp at Gonakudzingwa, in hot, desolate terrain in southeast Rhodesia near the border with Mozambique, and he remained in detention for ten years.

The internecine warfare continued until, in August 1964, the new Rhodesian Front leader, Ian Smith, banned the PCC (Zapu) and Zanu and rounded up every remaining nationalist leader, finally extinguishing the nationalist threat.


Mugabe applied to prison life the same discipline he had practised outside it. Initially he was moved from one prison to another, from Salisbury, to Wha Wha detention centre near Gwelo, and then to

Sikombela in Que Que. "It relieved the tedium but made us all so much more uncertain and frightened.... We were at the mercy of people we could never trust and from whom we had little or no information as to what was in store for us."

Arriving in Sikombela, a detention centre for Zanu detainees, Mugabe warned his colleagues not to expect early release and urged them to employ their time usefully in preparing for liberation. "These months, these years, however long it takes, must not be wasted," he told them. He organised study classes, acting as headmaster. Under Mugabe, Sikombela became a place of discipline and learning.

In 1966 Mugabe was taken back to Salisbury to a large communal cell, which he shared with Ndabaningi Sithole, Enos Nkala, and Edgar Tekere. He resumed his studies with fierce dedication, his books piled on both sides of his bed. "We never spent days without working," he recalled. "Every day, from Sunday to Saturday, mattered to us. We had to study." In the eight years he spent in Salisbury prison, he acquired three more degrees, in law and economics, by correspondence from London University. "I used to call him my Japanese student, he devoured books at such an amazing rate," one of his London tutors remembered. "He knew exactly what he wanted to do, so much so that it became quite a struggle to impress on him that, for the purpose of this exercise, I—not he—was the boss. He reminded me of Nehru—the same single-mindedness. I got the very clear impression that he was equipping his intellect for the tasks that lay ahead."

There was one episode from which Mugabe found it difficult to recover. One morning in December 1966 he was summoned to an interview room, where he found his sister, Sabina, in the company of a Rhodesian special branch officer. With tears running down her cheeks, Sabina told him that his son Nhamodzenyika had died from encephalitis at the home of Sally's parents in Ghana. Sally's sister, Esther, a doctor herself, saw the child in hospital. "If from the beginning, the baby had been strong, he might have survived. But the difficult conditions under which he was conceived and raised made him particularly susceptible to any infection."

Mugabe sobbed openly when he heard the news. "He was absolutely grief-stricken," recalled Tony Bradshaw, the special branch officer who was present. For days Mugabe remained inconsolable. He petitioned the government to be released temporarily from prison to travel to Ghana to mourn his son and comfort Sally. Bradshaw supported his petition, saying that Mugabe could be trusted to return to prison. But the government flatly refused. According to the Reverend Bill Clark, the chaplain-general of the prison service, who became one of Mugabe's closest confidants, he never forgot or forgave the government's attitude in this incident.

Sally too was devastated. Her most bitter thought, she said in an interview in 1983, was how little Mugabe had seen of his son. "All in all, my husband saw the baby as a tiny tot in Dar es Salaam, and then only for a few days when he visited Ghana for a meeting. He never had the chance to get to know his child, let alone play with him. I was better-off. I knew our little boy for three and a quarter years. His death is something we can never forget."

Sally later moved to London, earned a degree in home economics, and worked at the Runnymede Trust, spending her evenings in libraries copying out passages from books Mugabe needed for his studies. "In a sense I was in prison too when I was in Britain," she said.

By the end of the 1960s there was little sign that nationalist prisoners would ever be released. Ian Smith had declared unilateral independence from Britain in 1965, determined to entrench white rule for all time, without arousing any effective African opposition. Britain imposed economic sanctions but was otherwise anxious to negotiate a settlement. Its dispute with Smith was never over the question of granting independence to a white minority government, for the British government did not, in fact, find that prospect objectionable; it centred on whether the Rhodesian Front should make further constitutional concessions to win the right to independence. In 1966 Britain offered Smith a deal that would have postponed majority rule beyond the end of the century, but Smith was confident enough to believe he could obtain better terms. In 1967 Britain offered an even more favourable deal, but again Smith turned it down. In 1969 he introduced a new constitution that, in his own words, "sounded the death knell of the notion of majority rule" and "would entrench government in the hands of civilised Rhodesians for all time." Even then the British government still considered there was room for a deal. In 1971 the British foreign secretary, Sir Alec Douglas-Home, arrived in Salisbury bearing proposals so favourable to white Rhodesians that Smith accepted them. One constitutional expert, Professor Claire Palley, estimated that the agreement meant that the earliest year by which majority rule was likely to be achieved was 2035.

Nationalist leaders were brought out from their prison cells for Douglas-Home to hear their views, but they were given short shrift. When Mugabe told Douglas-Home that Africans were going to fight for their rights, the foreign secretary replied, "Apparently you have not been very successful in that."

African opposition to the deal, however, was strong enough to convince a British commission, set up to test public opinion, that the settlement terms were not acceptable to a majority of the population, and the deal fell through. Leading the opposition, Bishop Abel Muzorewa warned of the deep undercurrents of bitterness rising among the African population, "the repressed fear, restless silence, forced tolerance and hidden hatred." But far from paying heed to this new mood of defiance, Smith reacted vindictively, determined to make the black population pay for the lost opportunity of a settlement, enforcing discriminatory measures with ever greater vigour.

The guerrilla war began in earnest in the following year, launched by Zanu guerrillas infiltrating across the northern border with Mozambique, from rear bases in Zambia. South Africa responded by despatching large numbers of combat police to shore up the Rhodesian defence, regarding the Zambezi rather than the Limpopo as its own front line. But as the war dragged on in the northeast, the South Africans became increasingly disenchanted with Smith's intransigence. Zambia too was adversely affected by the reverberations of the war. In conjunction with other African leaders, the governments of Zambia and South Africa conspired to force on Smith and the nationalists their own plan for a Rhodesian settlement. The first that Mugabe knew of the scheme was when an envoy arrived from Lusaka in November 1974, interrupting his law examination.

Mugabe emerged from eleven years of imprisonment dedicated to the cause of revolutionary struggle. The death of his son had served only to make the cause even more important to him. He impressed people who met him with his soft-spoken demeanour, his broad intellect, and his articulate manner, but all this disguised a hardened and single-minded ambition.

The obstacles he faced were formidable. Whereas Mugabe was intent on resuming the guerrilla war under Zanu's banner, African leaders such as Kaunda and Nyerere were determined to achieve a united front between the rival factions of Zapu and Zanu. Not long after his arrival in Mozambique, Mugabe found himself placed under restriction in the port of Quelimane to prevent him from disrupting the formation of a combined guerrilla army, the Zimbabwe People's Army (Zipa), which African leaders wanted to construct from the ranks of Zapu and Zanu guerrillas.

Zipa eventually disintegrated after a series of bloody clashes between the two groups. Zanu too was beset for months by internal upheaval. Not until August 1977 did Mugabe manage to gain control of the army and the party.

The rivalry between Zanu and Zapu and their two guerrilla armies continued unabated. Ostensibly they were linked together as joint members of the Patriotic Front, but there was no trust between them. Mugabe's Zanla fought the brunt of the war in eastern Rhodesia, using bases in Mozambique; although supported by China, it was constantly short of food, clothing, and weapons. Nkomo's Zipra operated in areas of western Rhodesia, using bases in Zambia; supplied with substantial Russian aid, it kept most of its well-trained army in reserve, refusing to commit them to the war, prompting Zanla to suspect that they were being withheld for later use against its forces. To Mugabe's fury, Nkomo engaged in secret negotiations in 1978 with Smith, trying to achieve a settlement that would lead him to power separately.

At the Lancaster House conference in London in 1979, although they were still partners in the Patriotic Front, Mugabe and Nkomo barely concealed their differences. Each set up separate headquarters and retained separate spokesmen. While Mugabe was intent on pursuing the war to bring down not just white rule but Rhodesia's capitalist society with it, Nkomo was anxious that negotiations should succeed. At the age of sixty-two, in poor health, he saw no future for himself as a guerrilla leader in exile. Hugely relieved at the outcome at Lancaster House, he returned to Rhodesia in January 1980, pleaded for reconciliation with the whites, and instantly struck up a warm and comfortable relationship with Christopher Soames, giving him his full cooperation.

When it came to deciding how the Patriotic Front should fight the election, to Nkomo's dismay, Mugabe announced that Zanu would stand on its own. Once back in Rhodesia he made no attempt to get in touch with Nkomo and ignored messages suggesting they should meet. Nkomo complained to Soames. "I don't understand why Robert is doing this to me. He was my friend. We fought the war together. We've worked together. We've brought our forces together. And now Robert has cut me off." In private talks with

Soames, Nkomo urged him to penalise Mugabe and Zanu for intimidation.

The election results, providing Mugabe with a historic victory, dealt Nkomo a severe blow. He captured Matabeleland, gaining twenty seats, but nothing else. "I could not believe it," he recalled. He saw himself as the father figure of African nationalism in Rhodesia and seemed unable to grasp that over the years he had become no more than a regional leader of the Ndebele and Kalanga people. Invited by Soames to Government House soon after the results had been declared, he arrived close to tears, a shattered and broken man. "I am the Father of Zimbabwe; what have they done to me?" he said. "You give them one-man one-vote and look what they do with it! It has all come apart. It has all finished." He sat in Soames's private study dejectedly, almost dazed, bitter about Mugabe and his decision to fight the election separately. "We should have fought the election together. Mugabe let me down." Soames gave him a stiff drink. But Nkomo could not be consoled. In the following days he virtually shut himself away, refusing to put in an appearance even when British officials urged him to do so. Nkomo admitted: "I was deeply distressed."

When constructing his new government, Mugabe offered Nkomo the post of president, a ceremonial position with no executive power. "Robert told me that the office of president was the most exalted in the country, and constitutionally he was right," Nkomo recalled in his memoirs. "But personally he was entirely wrong. For me, acceptance of the presidency would have meant retreating into an official prison, deprived of my right to speak my mind and take a lead on matters of great national importance. I had spent too much of my life in prisons for that to be attractive, or even possible."

Eventually Nkomo settled for the ministry of home affairs, with control of the police. But there was a marked degree of resentment and suspicion between the two men that boded ill for the future.

At the independence celebrations in the football stadium in Salisbury, Nkomo and his wife, maFuyana, found themselves relegated to seats for lower-ranking guests:

> Behind the saluting base were the benches for the junior ministers, the party officials and the supporting cast. At the back of those rows, in the dark by the radio commentator's box, where the television cameras could not see us and our supporters in the crowd could not single us out for their applause, places were reserved for maFuyana and myself. In the stadiums of Zimbabwe I had so often stood up to address the crowds, and found the words to express what they wished to say but had not yet articulated. Now I was hidden away like something to be scared of. My wife could scarcely restrain her tears at this symbolic humiliation.

# [3]

# THE HONEYMOON

THE HONEYMOON of independence was brief but memorable. Mugabe settled comfortably into the prime minister's official residence, retaining the furniture that Ian Smith had once used, keeping even the placemats for breakfast with pictures of English pubs on them. Few changes were made. The head gardener now addressed the under-gardeners as "comrade" and bemoaned the switch from roses to vegetables: "Mr. Smith wouldn't have liked that." But otherwise the residence remained much as before.

In keeping with his promises about reconciliation, Mugabe strove to build a good working relationship with his former adversaries. Once it was clear on the eve of the announcement of the election results that he had won, Mugabe did not hesitate to invite Ian Smith round to his house for an exchange of views. "I was welcomed most courteously," wrote Smith in his memoirs. "He said he appreciated the vital need to retain the confidence of the white people so that they would continue to play their part in building the future of the country."

They parted cordially. "His appreciation seemed genuine, and as he escorted me to my car he expressed the wish that we would keep in contact," Smith said. "When I got back home, I said to Janet that I hoped it was not an hallucination. He behaved like a balanced, civilised Westerner, the antithesis of the communist gangster I had expected. If this was a true picture, then there could be hope instead of despair."

True to his word, Mugabe invited Smith over again a few days later. "We had a pleasant talk, just to keep me in the picture." They discussed Mugabe's decision to appoint two white ministers in the government. Another invitation came a week before independence. "I walked into my old office in Milton Building, received a courteous reception and was accompanied upstairs by his secretary. We discussed the settling-in process and the tremendous pressure of work."

In subsequent meetings, Smith found himself ever more impressed. "Once again I pondered to myself over the man's maturity, reasonableness and sense of fair play," he commented after a meeting in May. "A model of reason and fairness," he remarked in June.

Senior officials from the Rhodesian era whom Mugabe decided to retain were similarly impressed. Among them was Ken Flower, the head of the Central Intelligence Organisation (CIO), a secret police organisation, who had previously spent considerable effort trying to organise Mugabe's assassination. When Flower first called at his office, Mugabe suggested that they should meet regularly for a tête-à-tête. When they next met a few days later, Flower was anxious to explain about the various attempts the Rhodesians had made to kill Mugabe, to ensure that Mugabe was fully informed about his background. But Mugabe simply laughed. "Yes, but they all failed, otherwise we would not be here together," he remarked. "And do not expect me to applaud your failures."

Mugabe paused for a moment, then said, "As far as I have realised the position, we were trying to kill each other; that's what the war was about. What I'm concerned with now is that my public statements should be believed when I say I have drawn a line through the past. From now on we must trust each other if we are to work together for the benefit of the majority. I want people to believe in my policy of reconciliation and to respond accordingly."

Flower recalled in his memoirs,

> Walking back to my office in the hot sunshine, I felt as if a great burden had been lifted from my shoulders. Perhaps, at long last, the government servant and the politician could establish a worthwhile rapport. During the ten minutes or so that I walked, I reflected upon the various aspects of service with the four Prime Ministers with whom I had been closely associated and upon the man I was now serving. Robert Mugabe was emerging as someone with a greater capacity and determination to shape the country's destiny for the benefit of all its people than any of his four predecessors.

At a subsequent meeting, Flower volunteered to Mugabe the information that after the election he had handed over to South Africa control of an anti-government guerrilla force in Mozambique—Renamo—which the Rhodesian CIO had established and supplied for several years to counter Mozambique's support for Zanla. Mugabe, according to Flower, expressed no great surprise, indicating that he already knew that Flower was responsible for organising Renamo. But Flower was nonplussed when Mugabe mentioned that Mozambique's president, Samora Machel, had commended him as an adviser on whom he could rely.

"But Samora Machel and I have never met!" exclaimed Flower.

"He knows a lot about you," replied Mugabe, "otherwise he would not have recommended you to me."

"Does he know that I started [Renamo], which is causing him so much trouble?"

"Yes," said Mugabe, "and I imagine that is why he has so much respect for you."

Flower later reflected: "It was a strange experience working for an African leader whom whites had been taught to hate and whose assumption of power we had forecast to be catastrophic."

There were difficult adjustments to be made on both sides. Mugabe's minister for state security, Emmerson Mnangagwa, was a former Zanla guerrilla, trained in China, who had been captured after blowing up a railway locomotive, tortured, and then tried in court. But for his age, which was erroneously assessed as under sixteen, he would have been sentenced to death. His first action on the day he took over his department was to revisit the room in a police station where he had been tortured. White officers had hung him upside down by leg irons from butcher's hooks that ran along a track in the ceiling and then batted his suspended body back and forth on the track from one end of the room to the other. Mnangagwa found that not only were the butcher's hooks still in place but his former interrogators were now on his staff. They told him they had just been doing their jobs. He promised in return that they could start in independent Zimbabwe with a "clean slate."

The opening of parliament on May 15 aptly symbolised the mood of reconciliation. Mugabe and Smith walked into the chamber side by side, Mugabe leading in the column of government members of parliament (MPs), Smith at the head of a line of twenty white MPs elected separately by the white community, in accordance with the terms of the Lancaster House agreement. Accompanying them were a bevy of military figures, the elite of the old military establishment together with the former commanders of Zanla and Zipra. After the ceremony Mugabe invited Smith for a chat. Smith departed once again feeling reassured. "So all around it did seem to me that Zimbabwe had much going its way and that we were heading for fair weather."

As well as being represented by their own MPs, the white community was gratified by the presence in government of two white ministers specially appointed by Mugabe: David Smith, a former Rhodesian Front minister, and Dennis Norman, a former president of the commercial farmers' union. During the election campaign, Mugabe had taken the trouble to arrange meetings with the leaders of industry, commerce, mining, and agriculture, making a favourable impression on them. He met the farmers first.

"They were amazed," recalled Norman. "Was this the ogre they had heard about? Here they were seeing a man who was articulate, warm, anxious for a full understanding of how the mixed economy he was about to inherit worked. 'My knowledge is limited.' He and his colleagues were good listeners, there was no need to argue a case. 'Could our staffs discuss the next steps?' We were delighted to agree." After consulting Lord Soames, Mugabe asked Norman to become minister of agriculture.

As a result of Mugabe's careful patronage, white farmers, nervous and depressed by the election results, soon rebounded with confidence. One of the most privileged groups in the country, numbering no more than 6,000 in all, they owned almost half of the land and two-thirds of the best land, all of which was protected from expropriation under the terms of the Lancaster House agreement, which Mugabe insisted he would observe for its full period of ten years. For some farmers the relief of no longer being at war was sufficient reward. Just after the election results were announced, the wife of a Mount Darwin farmer described her new world as "heaven—sheer bliss. We can actually sleep through the whole night." Moreover, in its first two years Zimbabwe was further blessed with good rains and record harvests. And when Dennis Norman, in his new role as minister, won large increases in the producer price of maize, many white farmers became ardent supporters of the new government. "Good old Bob!" they cheered.

For whites in general there were many immediate benefits. No longer did they face military call-up, economic sanctions, or petrol rationing. Now they were free to take up old leisure pursuits abandoned during the war: trips to the eastern highlands, boating on Lake Kariba, weekend game viewing. As well as owning most commercial farmland, they dominated commerce, industry, and banking; possessed a virtual monopoly of high-level skills; and retained for the most part considerable property and personal wealth. In the economic boom that followed the end of the war—growth of 24 percent in two years—the whites were major beneficiaries.

For many whites, however, the advent of an avowedly Marxist black government was more than they could stomach, and a steady exodus began, mainly to South Africa, the last haven of white rule. Most left complaining that standards in education, health, urban services, and policing were bound to deteriorate. Some were worried at the rate of Africanisation of jobs affecting not only their own job prospects but their children's. There was widespread irritation at the way in which radio and television, once the vehicles for Rhodesian Front propaganda, were swiftly turned into the propaganda arm of Zanu-PF, with frequent disparaging references made to "racist" whites. During 1980 some 17,000 whites emigrated, about one-tenth of the white population. Among them were retired civil servants, former soldiers and policemen disgruntled at the outcome of the election, and skilled artisans and professional people: doctors, accountants, teachers, and nurses.

On the international stage Zimbabwe was accorded star status. One country after another lined up to help the new government make a success of its multiracial venture. "We are the darling of the world," Mugabe told a meeting of white farmers, "and since we are on honeymoon and honeymoons don't always last too long, we ought to take advantage of it!"

The British government provided a military assistance team to help integrate guerrilla forces with the old Rhodesian army, earning Mugabe's praise. Britain also financed the start of a land redistribution programme. Indeed, Mugabe cultivated a closer relationship with Britain than with any other country, putting all past disputes behind him. "I think we were never really hostile to Britain as such. When we fought the war here, of course we said we were fighting colonialism and imperialism. But we were never really hostile to the British people—and we are independent and there is no quarrel with Britain."

Other Western states were also generous with aid. The United States provided Zimbabwe with a three-year aid package of US $225 million, describing its relationship as a "warm embrace." At an international donors conference in March 1981, Zimbabwe gained promises of £636 million, bringing the total aid pledged in one year of independence to nearly £900 million. A wave of aid workers and foreign expatriates arrived to help build the new state. Western governments were hopeful in particular that a stable and prosperous Zimbabwe might help to ease the process of change in South Africa, where apartheid was in force. "The success of Zimbabwe's experiment with nationhood sends a clear message to the region and the world about the prospects of lasting negotiated settlements in southern Africa and of reconciliation among the region's strife-torn peoples," said the senior U.S. official for African affairs, Frank Wisner.

Mugabe's own attitude towards South Africa was initially pragmatic. At independence he offered South Africa peaceful coexistence but nevertheless pledged his support for African nationalist movements such as the African National Congress. "We are against apartheid and have a duty to assist our brothers and sisters," he said. He emphasised, though, that the support given would be primarily diplomatic. He would not allow them to establish military bases or training camps in Zimbabwe. However, to the dismay of the whites, he also announced that all sporting links with South Africa would cease. The president of the Rugby Union, Des van Jaarsveldt, urged the government to reconsider: An entire way of life was at stake, a tradition of competitions stretching back to 1905. But Mugabe was adamant.

Bolstered by offers of foreign assistance, the government embarked on ambitious programmes to extend education and health services to the entire population. But although Mugabe still spoke of the goal of socialist transformation, the government's budgetary policies were conservative. Mugabe asked Africans to be patient. "We shall proceed to bring about changes but changes in a realistic manner," he said. Much attention was paid to the need to attract foreign investors and to pursue development on capitalist lines before moving on to socialist measures. "We recognise that the economic structure of this country is based on capitalism, and that whatever ideas we have, we must build on that. Modifications can only take place in a gradual way."

Few changes, in fact, directly affected the white community. Statues of Cecil Rhodes were taken down; the main avenues in central Salisbury were renamed in honour of Presidents Machel and Nyerere; Cecil Square, the park in the centre of Salisbury where the Union Jack had first been raised, was renamed Africa Unity Square; and in 1982 Salisbury itself became Harare. But this was hardly the stuff of revolution that the whites had once feared and, indeed, Mugabe had promised.

What shocks occurred were relatively minor. In July 1980 General Walls gave notice that he intended to resign as head of the new Joint High Command. He had accepted the position reluctantly, and he had since become aggrieved by Mugabe's refusal to agree to his promotion from lieutenant-general to full general, a rank that not even Smith had countenanced. The matter passed swiftly enough at the time. But in the following month Walls, while still serving as commander, gave a television interview in which he disclosed that earlier in the year he had asked British prime minister Margaret Thatcher to annul the election results and criticised her for not doing so.

The damage done to the government's attempts at partnership was severe, as Ken Flower, Mugabe's intelligence chief, noted in his diary: "By criticising Mrs. Thatcher for not reversing the election results he has let the whole world know that he resents serving Mugabe, or is serving him under false pretences."

Flower subsequently discussed the issue at length with Mugabe. "Had two hours alone with Mugabe yesterday, talking mostly about Peter Walls," he recorded in his diary. "There will be no recovery there. Mugabe believes that Peter betrayed him: having sworn a personal loyalty but still living in the past and not really serving him as Prime Minister, although Mugabe described how he had done everything he could to win his friendship."

Another shock occurred as a result of the activities of one of Mugabe's most trusted lieutenants and closest friends, Edgar Tekere. They had spent years together in prison, escaped together to Mozambique in 1975, and survived the turmoil of struggling for the leadership of Zanu in exile. When Mugabe became party leader, Tekere was elected secretary-general, third in the party hierarchy. Yet Tekere was prone to wild and reckless conduct. As a minister in the new government, he soon achieved notoriety for his controversial outbursts. In July 1980, harbouring a grievance against the Anglican Church, he attacked prominent white Anglican churchmen and accused the church of being "an instrument of oppression." His remarks, broadcast at length on television, caused outrage amongst white viewers.

The following month, accompanied by seven armed bodyguards, Tekere led an attack on a white farmhouse near Salisbury in which a sixty-eight-year-old white farmer was killed. During his trial for murder, Tekere did not deny leading the attack but argued that he was acting as Mugabe's "task man," foiling a coup being planned on the farm. He claimed immunity under the provisions of a piece of wartime legislation, the Indemnity and Compensation Act, that Smith had used to grant immunity to government ministers and people acting on their orders in good faith to suppress terrorism. On the basis of this defence, Tekere was acquitted. Even though Mugabe subsequently dropped him from the cabinet, to many whites the incident served to confirm their deep misgivings about the consequences of black rule.

The aura of goodwill that accompanied independence soon evaporated. Not only Tekere but several other ministers took to criticising the white community in speeches that were reported prominently by the government-controlled media. In his private talks with Mugabe, Ian Smith protested time and again at what he called "the ongoing campaign of recrimination against our white community." Mugabe's response initially, according to Smith, was to promise to deal with the matter. "Somewhat naively, he said he could not understand why people did not accept his word and ignore wild statements. In reply, I informed him that the wild statements received publicity every day, while his word was never heard by the general public." As the attacks continued, Smith became sceptical about Mugabe's assurances. "I hoped he was not resorting to the tactic of feigning ignorance, and passing the buck to his various ministers when in fact they were following his instructions." In 1981 Smith tackled Mugabe in private about his open support for a one-party state, pointing out the adverse effect it had on foreign investors. It was their last meeting. "He was obviously displeased, and our parting, unlike previous occasions, was cool. He stood his distance."

In parliament, Smith's MPs adopted an increasingly abrasive attitude, carping at the government at every available opportunity. One white MP, a former special forces officer, urged ministers to go back to the bush "where they belong." Another, a former air force pilot, taunted the government by claiming that the Rhodesian security forces had "never lost a battle, or even a skirmish" and took pleasure in describing his holidays in "racist South Africa." Smith weighed in, suggesting that the new government should display proper gratitude for the benefits of ninety years of white rule. He became perpetually gloomy, telling all and sundry that Zimbabwe was sliding towards a one-party Marxist dictatorship.

What finally put an end to the honeymoon period was the growing confrontation with South Africa. For years the South Africans had bolstered Smith's war effort, determined to prevent Rhodesia falling into the hands of communist guerrillas. With similar zeal they had put their weight behind Bishop Muzorewa's coalition government, throwing large sums of money into his election campaign. Mugabe's election victory confounded their expectations. Instead of a moderate black government on their doorstep, they now had a Marxist government in control. When taken together with Angola and Mozambique, this meant that a trio of avowedly Marxist states lay across their northern frontier, all committed to the cause of African liberation.

The South Africans moved swiftly to counter this new threat. They recruited into their own defence force some 5,000 former Rhodesian military personnel, including entire special force units such as the Selous Scouts, and set about establishing a network of agents, informers, spies, and saboteurs inside Zimbabwe, finding a large number of serving officers in the army, air force, police, and the CIO only too ready to help. Among the senior officers they recruited was Geoffrey Price, a CIO chief in charge of Mugabe's close security. The South Africans also took control of Renamo, the Mozambique rebel group that Ken Flower had handed over to them.

South Africa's principal objective was to keep Zimbabwe in a weak and defensive position, to destabilise it to ensure that it presented neither a security threat nor an example of a stable African state. Economic disruption by blocking trade routes was used at first, but it was not long before military activists went to work.

In July 1981 a prominent South African nationalist, Joe Gqabi, the chief representative of the African National Congress in Zimbabwe, was assassinated in Salisbury. As subsequent investigations showed, he was the target of an undercover defence force unit led by a former Rhodesian policeman working in collaboration with serving members of the CIO. The following month, a huge armoury at Inkomo military barracks, near Harare, was blown up by a white army engineer working for the South Africans. From mid-1981 on, Renamo forces under South African control began attacks on the railway, road, and pipeline linking Zimbabwe to the Mozambique port of Beira.

Then in December 1981 a massive bomb blast tore apart Zanu-PF headquarters in central Salisbury, killing seven people in an adjoining bakery and injuring 124 Christmas shoppers in the street. Mugabe and other members of Zanu's central committee had been scheduled to meet in the conference room there, but the meeting had been delayed. Mugabe was convinced he was the target of the attack and blamed it on South Africa and disaffected whites in Zimbabwe acting in collusion with South Africa.

The "honeymoon," he said, was over. "What baffles my government is that reactionary and counter-revolutionary elements, because of their treason and crimes against humanity in Zimbabwe we could have put before a firing squad, but which we decided to forgive, have hardly repented." Instead of working for national reconciliation, "they have in practice rejected it and are acting in collusion with South Africa to harm our racial relations, to destroy our unity, to sabotage our economy, and to overthrow the popularly elected government I lead."

He went on to warn, "In these circumstances, where those with a criminal record continue not only to display it as a heroic achievement, but also add to it by committing fresh crimes... my government is bound to revise its policy of national reconciliation and take definite steps to mete out harsh punishment to this clan of unrepentant and criminal savages."

Mugabe broadened his attack on whites to include not just spies and saboteurs but the white community as a whole, focusing his anger on the wealth they continued to enjoy. After eighteen months of independence, he said, white racial attitudes had not changed; they continued to scold, beat, and abuse their workers. "It is the blood and sweat of the workers that has made these people millionaires. They have sucked the blood of their workers like vampires so that they can board expensive aeroplanes and go on long holidays." It was no longer acceptable that "the very bourgeoisie which only yesterday enjoyed political power and used it to oppress the Zimbabwean people...continues to have a monopoly on Zimbabwe's economic power." That, he said, must be broken.

What lingering hopes there were for racial harmony gave way to mutual mistrust and suspicion. One incident after another compounded the problem. A group of middle-aged whites, ten of them women, were leaving an army barracks after playing a lawn bowls match on the barracks' green when they were stopped at the gate by a high-ranking black officer, ordered out of their cars at gunpoint, and taken to cells where they were interrogated and accused of being South African agents.

An elderly white MP, Wally Stuttaford, was arrested under emergency powers in December 1981, accused of plotting to overthrow the government, and held incommunicado. During interrogation he was subjected to hours of kicking, punching, and forced exercise and had his arms, hands, and ankles crushed until he screamed with pain and begged for mercy. He was not charged, and no evidence against him was ever produced. In parliament in January 1982, Ian Smith complained about Stuttaford's continued detention without trial, much to the fury of black MPs who themselves had been detained by Smith using the same emergency powers. "When you jailed us, you took your time," shouted Eddison Zvogbo, a government minister. "We were inside for ten years and you are complaining because Stuttaford has been inside for thirty days." A review tribunal found Stuttaford's imprisonment illegal, but the government ignored this and continued to detain him. While in prison he successfully sued the government and CIO officers for assault and torture, winning record damages. But Mugabe said he would ignore the award as it was "a waste of the nation's money." When, seven months later, Stuttaford was brought to court charged with plotting the violent overthrow of the government, the case against him swiftly collapsed.

In July 1982 the South Africans struck again with deadly effect, destroying thirteen aircraft in a raid on Thornhill, Zimbabwe's main air force base near Gweru. The raid was carried out by an assault team of three Rhodesian saboteurs recruited by South African military intelligence, working in conjunction with a white air force officer stationed at the base who had provided them with vital intelligence. Casting round for culprits, black police investigators arrested several senior air force officers, including the deputy commander, Air Vice-Marshall Hugh Slatter. Slatter was denied access to lawyers, held incommunicado, and tortured with electric shocks until he admitted involvement in the raid. In August 1983, at the end of their trial, a black judge, Enoch Dumbutshena, concluded that the case against Slatter and five other air force officers rested entirely on confessions obtained by torture and accordingly acquitted them. But while they were embracing their wives and families, the airmen were all re-arrested, prompting an international outcry.

Mugabe did not attempt to deny that the airmen had been tortured. "Unfortunately, our interrogators used irregular methods. We admit they were irregular. They did use torture." But he was not troubled that torture had been used. Nor did he see any reason why the airmen should not be re-detained after their acquittal. The information obtained from them was not necessarily incorrect, he said. The government believed they were South African agents, and it would not be "responsible" to let them "float about committing acts of destruction."

Taken to task over the issue at a press conference in Dublin, Mugabe questioned the motives behind Western protests at the detentions. "Why is there so much concern about these men? They are not the only ones in detention. Is it because they are white, because they are Mrs. Thatcher's kith and kin?"

He then spelled out his dislike for a legal system that rejected evidence obtained by ill-treatment: "The law of evidence and the criminal procedure we have inherited is a stupid ass. It's one of those principles born out of the stupidity of some of the procedures of colonial times."

Slatter and his colleagues were eventually released. But Mugabe's standing abroad was severely damaged by his overt contempt for legal procedures. The London *Times* commented: "Mr. Mugabe's government substitutes its writ for the courts and is scornful of 'legal technicalities'. Thus the protection all Zimbabwean citizens deserve from arbitrary arrest and imprisonment without due process disappears; liberty depends on the whim of the an individual."

The white exodus gathered momentum. Within three years of independence, about half of the white population emigrated. What was left was a rump of 100,000 whites who retreated into their own world of clubs, sporting activities, and comfortable living.

As recalcitrant as ever, Ian Smith portrayed himself as the defender of this "white tribe" grumbling constantly about government incompetence, corruption, and other threats to their well-being. During a trip abroad to Britain and the United States in November 1982 he painted a dismal picture of Zimbabwe as a country in dire straits, heading fast for one-party Marxist rule.

On his return, the government retaliated. Police raided an art exhibition in Harare that Smith was attending as a guest of honour, rounded up all the guests, and took them to a police station for questioning. "We were taken underground where all the drunks and prostitutes congregated," recalled Smith. A police spokesman later explained that they had been investigating a suspected illegal political meeting. The following week Smith's passport was withdrawn, according to a government minister, because of his "political bad manners and hooliganism" in criticising Zimbabwe while abroad. A few days later, while Smith was on his 6,000-acre farm, 200 miles southwest of Harare, twelve policemen arrived to search the premises. "They went through everything with a finetooth comb, through drawers and wardrobes, under mattresses, under the floor, under pots and pans, through outside storerooms and barns. They even asked our old vegetable gardener if I had ever dug a hole and buried something." The police left after five hours, taking personal papers and a diary with them. "It's all part of the game to intimidate me and so demoralise the whites," said Smith. Two days later the police called at the farm again and took Smith to Harare, where they searched his town house. On a third visit the police took away firearms used on the farm.

A majority of Smith's white colleagues in parliament disapproved of his confrontational manner, preferring cooperation with the government, and they deserted his party to sit as independent members. But Smith remained obdurate. Who but his own party, he asked, would "stand up for the rights and the beliefs of the whites?"

In the election for the white seats in parliament in 1985, the last before their seven-year term under the Lancaster House agreement expired, Smith was vindicated. His party, the Conservative Alliance of Zimbabwe, gained fifteen of twenty seats.

Seeing their victory as a betrayal, Mugabe reacted with fury, denouncing Smith and the "racists" who had voted for him and threatening reprisals. The trust shown to the white community at independence had been completely undeserved, he said:

> The voting has shown that they have not repented in any way. They still cling to the past and support the very man...who created a series of horrors against the people of Zimbabwe. We wish to make it very clear that it is going to be very hard for the racists of this country.... Those whites who have not accepted the reality of a political order in which the Africans set the pace will have to leave the country. We are working with those whites who want to work with us. But the rest will have to find a new home.

Speaking in chiShona, he promised, "We will kill those snakes among us, we will smash them completely."

Not since the war years had Mugabe used such language. It was a glimpse of a man unremitting against opposition. His first victims, however, were not whites, but the Ndebele and Kalanga.

# [4]

## *GUKURAHUNDI*

THE RISK OF A second civil war following independence was ever present from the moment the new flag of Zimbabwe was raised. The election campaign, fought with so much aggression, had intensified all the distrust and animosity that Mugabe's Zanu-PF and Nkomo's Zapu harboured for each other. Their two guerrilla armies remained potential adversaries. Although strenuous efforts were made, under British supervision, to integrate them into a new defence force as rapidly as possible, the process was fraught with difficulty. Nkomo's Zipra army, numbering some 20,000 men, had been recruited mainly from Matabeleland, spoke in Sindebele, and had been trained largely as a regular force, with air and armoured units. Mugabe's Zanla army, twice as large, had been recruited from Shona-speaking areas and was more loosely structured for guerrilla warfare. Zipra forces, owing allegiance to Nkomo and Zapu, were disgruntled by the election results, leading Zanla to suspect they might attempt insurrection.

The intense rivalry between the two groups soon affected the workings of the coalition government. Nkomo maintained that his party deserved more than four of the twenty-three seats in the cabi-

net and complained that Zanu-PF was making government decisions on its own without consulting its partners. Zanu-PF ministers
questioned Zapu's participation in the cabinet in the first place, de-
riding Zipra's contribution to the war effort. They talked avidly of
the need for a one-party state, hoping for complete control.
Scarcely a day went by without one side or the other engaging in
personal invective.

There was an immediate source of friction over the activities of
renegade guerrillas from both armies who had deserted their camps
and taken up banditry. Zanla guerrillas went on the rampage in the
northeast. But Mugabe chose to emphasise the role of Zipra deserters. While stopping short of accusing Zapu's leadership of responsibility, he claimed that "organised bands of Zipra followers" were
"refusing to recognise the sovereignty of the government" and suggested they were motivated by disaffection over the election results.
"If those who have suffered defeat adopt the unfortunate and inde-
fensible attitude that defies and rejects the verdict of the people,
then reconciliation between the victor and vanquished is impossible," he said in June 1980. Nkomo called Mugabe's comments "a
slap in the face." It was, he said, "a tragedy that such an outrageous
statement should have been made." No one in Zapu had flouted
government authority.

Mugabe's closest colleagues, Edgar Tekere and Enos Nkala, were
spoiling for a fight, and with utter recklessness, openly talked of the
need to "crush" Zapu. Nkala, himself a Ndebele, claimed that the
deserters were "Ndebeles who were calling for a second war of liberation," and said they should be "shot down." He called Nkomo a
"self-appointed Ndebele king" who needed to be "crushed." Tekere
went further: "Nkomo and his guerrillas are germs in the country's
wounds and they will have to be cleaned up with iodine. The patient
will have to scream a bit." Mugabe made no attempt to distance
himself from these remarks. To Zapu and Zipra alike, it appeared
that Mugabe was bent on provoking a showdown.

Amid these tense conditions, large groups of Zanla and Zipra guerrillas were moved from rural camps to urban centres—Chitungwiza, near Harare, and Entumbane, a suburb of Bulawayo—in an attempt to stop rural banditry and to provide them with better accommodation. In Chitungwiza they were housed in separate locations no more than a mile apart. As a warning of what was to come, a gun battle between rival factions broke out there in October, lasting thirty minutes.

The first major clash erupted the following month in Entumbane. It started after Enos Nkala arrived in Bulawayo to address a political rally there and launched into a vitriolic tirade against Nkomo and Zapu. "As from today Zapu has become the enemy of Zanu-PF," he said. "The time has come for Zanu-PF to flex its muscles. Our supporters must now form vigilante committees for those who want to challenge us. There must be a general mobilisation of our supporters. Organise yourselves into small groups in readiness to challenge Zapu on its home ground. If it means a few blows, we shall deliver them."

After the rally, rival party supporters clashed in the streets. In Entumbane, where Zipra and Zanla had been housed in adjacent camps, guerrillas fought a pitched battle that lasted two days. The incident led to increased tension and distrust at other bases across the country, including newly integrated units of the defence force, and convinced many guerrillas that further conflict was inevitable.

Despite the risks, Mugabe continued to force the issue. In January 1981, in a cabinet reshuffle, he demoted Nkomo, removing him from police responsibilities and giving him an insignificant post as minister in charge of the public service. "The whole thing is a complete violation of our understanding that Zapu and Zanu-PF should [share security portfolios]," protested Nkomo. "Mugabe made the move without consultation or negotiation. I object to this." He warned of the possibility of unrest, but Mugabe paid no heed.

In February 1981 an outbreak of fighting in a newly integrated battalion stationed at Ntabazinduna, north of Bulawayo, spread to Entumbane and to other bases. When Zipra reinforcements tried to break through to Entumbane, Mugabe had to rely on old Rhodesian army units to stop them. More than 300 people died. In the aftermath of this second round of fighting, large numbers of Zipra soldiers, fearing for their safety, deserted their units, taking their weapons with them. On both sides, arms were cached.

Mugabe's strategy henceforth was to have fearful consequences for Matabeleland. He turned to North Korea, a brutal communist dictatorship, for assistance in training a new army brigade with the specific remit to deal with internal dissidents. A secret agreement was signed in October 1980, but it was not until August 1981 that Mugabe disclosed that a team of 106 North Korean instructors had arrived in Zimbabwe to train the new force. Nkomo was immediately suspicious and accused Mugabe of raising "a special partisan army divorced from the national army" for the "possible imposition of a one-party state."

By early 1982, once the new defence force had completed its integration exercise, Mugabe felt secure enough to stage a split with Nkomo. The pretext was arms caches. On February 7 Mugabe announced that an arms cache had been discovered on Ascot Farm, twenty miles north of Bulawayo, a property belonging to a Zapu-owned company with two directors, one of whom was Nkomo. Ascot Farm was part of a portfolio of properties bought by Zapu after independence with funds mostly provided by former Zipra soldiers, who invested their demobilisation payments and pensions; the portfolio included an assortment of businesses, hotels, butcheries, and farms, which were used as resettlement schemes for ex-combatants. Among the arms found on Ascot Farm were assault rifles, mortars, missiles, anti-aircraft weapons, and land mines. Raids on several other Zapu farms turned up more arms dumps. Mugabe claimed that the arms finds were clear evidence of plans by Zapu's leadership to instigate a military coup. "These people were planning to overthrow and take over the government," he declared. The farms they had bought were a mere cover for hiding weapons.

The existence of arms caches held by Zanla and Zipra had been a recognised problem since independence. Zipra troops returning from Zambia in 1980 had brought with them huge arsenals, which they retained in their own camps while waiting to be integrated into the new defence force. As a result of the clashes between Zanla and Zipra guerrillas, a large amount of weaponry had been cached. According to Zipra commanders, the caches were established not because they planned a coup but for Zipra's own protection. Their existence was common knowledge. In early 1982, an ad hoc committee met to discuss how best to deal with the problem; it consisted of Mugabe and Mnangagwa, his security minister, and Nkomo and Dumiso Dabengwa, Zipra's former chief of intelligence. But before the committee had resolved on a course of action, Mugabe made his move, announcing the arms find on Ascot Farm.

At a party rally a week later, all his festering resentment against Nkomo came tumbling out in public. He likened Nkomo's role in the cabinet to having "a cobra in the house" and went on: "The only way to deal effectively with a snake is to strike and destroy its head. How else can I describe a man who we supposed was our friend and whom we invited to be part of the government when we could have formed a Zanu-PF government without him?" Nkomo, he said, had a long history of failures: At secret talks with Smith in the 1970s and at the Lancaster House conference in 1979, he had tried "to sell the country to our oppressors." During the guerrilla war, Zapu had held back its forces "to fight in a final struggle to overthrow Zanu-PF government if it came to power." Mugabe said his heart had been "torn to pieces" by the discovery that Nkomo and Zapu were working behind the scenes to "create further strife, tears and bloodshed."

Nkomo was duly sacked from the government; his party's businesses, farms, and properties were seized, ruining thousands of

Zipra ex-combatants who had invested money in them; and two former Zipra leaders, Dumiso Dabengwa and General Lookout Masuku, the deputy commander of the national army, were arrested and subsequently tried for treason and illegal possession of weapons. Although acquitted in 1983, they were immediately re-detained. Nkomo denied all Mugabe's accusations. "The arms were not the real issue," he said. "This was the trigger-point of a political move against me, for pushing ahead the one-party state and for removing certain obstacles."

The position of ex-Zipra soldiers in the national army became increasingly perilous. They had lost their main representatives in the government and in the army. Now they faced reprisals from ex-Zanla soldiers. Many were killed, beaten, or otherwise victimised. Hundreds fled, taking their arms with them. Groups of ex-Zipra "dissidents," as they were called, roamed Matabeleland, robbing stores and holding up buses. Their attacks spread to isolated farmhouses and villages. White farmers found themselves reverting back to war-time habits, carrying weapons, wary of ambushes; several were killed. Six foreign tourists were abducted and murdered. In Harare, Mugabe's official residence in Chancellor Avenue and Enos Nkala's house in the suburbs were attacked by ex-Zipra gunmen.

The growing lawlessness in Matabeleland provided South Africa with an opportunity to meddle in the conflict. White CIO officers working clandestinely for the South Africans had already managed to fan the flames of suspicion and mistrust during the controversy over arms caches, providing Mugabe with exaggerated reports of their significance. From mid-1982 the South Africans began to recruit and train ex-Zipra combatants at a base in the northern Transvaal, reinforcing them with black soldiers from the Rhodesian security forces who had previously crossed the border after independence to avoid Mugabe's rule. The operation was given the name Operation Mute. From late 1982 on, small groups infiltrated into Matabeleland, adding to the mayhem. No more than a hundred men were involved, but in the terminology the South Africans used at the time, they were enough "to keep the pot boiling."

Mugabe deployed army and police reinforcements to stamp out dissident activity, giving them licence to detain people at will. Local interrogation centres were set up by the CIO. Strict curfew regulations were enforced. Using legislation similar to that adopted by Smith during the war, Mugabe granted freedom from prosecution to government officials and security forces for all actions provided they were taken "for the purposes of or in connection with the preservation of the security for Zimbabwe." In a speech to parliament in 1982, he warned, "Some of the measures we shall take are measures which will be extra-legal. . . . An eye for an eye and an ear for an ear may not be adequate in our circumstances. We might very well demand two ears for one ear and two eyes for one eye."

The real culprit behind the banditry, according to Mugabe, was Zapu. It was acting in league with South African–backed groups infiltrating Matabeleland, which Mugabe dubbed "super-Zapu." Furthermore, he claimed, the local population was actively supporting the dissidents. Thus the conflict in Matabeleland, as Mugabe portrayed it, was an attempt by an alliance of Zapu, the dissidents, and South Africa to overthrow the government. Nkomo denied all the accusations and repeatedly condemned the dissidents. But Mugabe was intent on outright repression.

By the end of 1982 Mugabe was ready to unleash his new army brigade: 5 Brigade. Trained by the North Koreans, it was different from any other army unit. Its troops wore different uniforms, with distinctive red berets. It used different equipment, transport, and weaponry. Its codes and radios were incompatible with other units. It was drawn almost entirely from Shona-speaking ex-Zanla forces loyal to Mugabe. Its chain of command bypassed the intermediate levels observed by the rest of the army, answering directly to Mugabe's army commanders.

Mugabe was explicit about its purpose. "They [5 Brigade] were trained by the North Koreans because we wanted one arm of the army to have a political orientation which stems from our philosophy as Zanu-PF," he said. He called the new brigade *Gukurahundi*, a Shona word defined as meaning the rain that blows away the chaff before the spring rains. Mugabe had used the term during the war, naming 1979 as *Gore reGukurahundi*, "the Year of the People's Storm," signifying the culmination of the people's struggle against white rule. In Matabeleland, *Gukurahundi* acquired a more sinister meaning; there it was interpreted as "the sweeping away of rubbish."

In December 1982 Mugabe attended 5 Brigade's Passing Out Parade, presenting the brigade colours, a flag emblazoned with the word *Gukurahundi*, to its commander, Colonel Perence Shiri, a former Zanla guerrilla commander. "From today onwards," Colonel Shiri told his troops. "I want you to start dealing with dissidents."

The dissident problem was far smaller than the government contended. At the time, the number of dissidents in Matabeleland North was no more than about 200. Throughout Matabeleland as a whole, their numbers never exceeded more than 400 at the peak of dissident activity. They had no coherent policy or aims other than to commit random sabotage. Some were ex-Zipra soldiers; others had no military training; some were ordinary criminals. They had little popular support and their reputation for murder, rape, and coercion made them even less popular.

Government ministers, however, portrayed the dissidents as well-supplied and well-organised fighting units and constantly exaggerated the level of their activities when it suited them. Without ever producing any evidence, they continued to assert that Zapu and the dissidents were one and the same. Addressing a rally in Matabeleland South in February 1983, Enos Nkala told the crowd that if they continued to support dissidents and Zapu "you shall die or be sent to prison."

From the moment it was deployed in Matabeleland North at the end of January 1983, 5 Brigade waged a campaign of beatings, arson, and mass murder deliberately targeted at the civilian population. Villagers were rounded up and marched long distances to a central location, such as a school, where they were harangued and beaten for hours on end. The beatings were often followed by public executions. The main targets initially were former Zipra soldiers or Zapu officials whose names were read out from lists, but often victims were chosen at random and included women. Villagers were then forced to sing songs in the Shona language praising Zanu-PF while dancing on the mass graves of their families and fellow villagers killed and buried minutes earlier.

Massacres occurred. On February 6 fifty-two villagers were shot in a village in Lupane district, mostly in small groups in the vicinity of their own homes. On March 5 fifty-five men and women were shot on the banks of the Ciwale River. On March 9 twenty-six villagers in Mkhonyeni, including women and children, were herded into huts and burned alive while the rest of the village was forced to watch. Within the space of six weeks, at least 2,000 civilians were killed, hundreds of homesteads were destroyed, and tens of thousands of civilians were beaten. In addition, 5 Brigade imposed stringent curfews, banned all forms of transport, closed shops, and blocked drought relief supplies for villagers facing starvation. To all intents and purposes, it acted as an army of occupation, committing atrocities at will. The scale of violence was far worse than anything that had occurred during the Rhodesian war.

None of this was reported by the government-controlled press, radio, or television. Foreign press reports on the violence were dismissed as fabrications. Evidence of atrocities collected by churchmen, doctors, and aid agencies and submitted to the government was ignored. On March 16, a Catholic delegation including two bishops and the chairman of the Commission for Justice and Peace presented Mugabe with a comprehensive dossier containing damning evidence of 5 Brigade atrocities. They also included a pastoral statement drawn up by the Catholic Bishops' Conference, which they intended to deliver on the forthcoming Easter weekend. The statement accused the army of conducting "a reign of terror" in Matabeleland, including "wanton killings, woundings, beatings, burnings and rapings." It had "brought about the maiming and death of hundreds and hundreds of innocent people who are neither dissidents nor collaborators."

Mugabe's response was to refute all allegations of atrocities. He described the Catholic bishops as "sanctimonious prelates" who were "playing to the international gallery." He queried whether they were their own masters or "mere megaphonic agents of their external manipulative masters," adding: "In those circumstances, their allegiance and loyalty to Zimbabwe becomes extremely questionable." He continued: "The Church of Zimbabwe, whatever the denomination, must abandon forever the tendency or temptation to play marionette for foreign so-called parent churches whose interests and perspectives may, and often will be, at variance with the best interests of the people of our country." It should "attune itself to the realities of the new Zimbabwe."

Mugabe was blunt about his approach to counter-insurgency. "We have to deal with this problem quite ruthlessly," he told an audience in rural Matabeleland. "Don't cry if your relatives get killed in the process.... Where men and women provide food for the dissidents, when we get there we eradicate them. We do not differentiate who we fight because we can't tell who is a dissident and who is not."

Government ministers continued their attacks on Nkomo. Enos Nkala described him as "public enemy No. 1" and declared "Zapu must be eliminated." In March, while Nkomo was away from home spending the night with relatives, members of 5 Brigade arrived at his Bulawayo house, ransacked it, and then shot dead his driver and two other staff members. Nkomo decided to flee, escaping across the border to Botswana and then seeking refuge in Britain. He spent the third anniversary of Zimbabwe's independence in a rented two-room flat off the Edgware Road in London.

The *Gukurahundi* campaign continued relentlessly for month after month. Villagers and children were forced to attend Zanu-PF rallies, which sometimes lasted for entire weekends and frequently involved public beatings. Possessing a Zanu-PF card became essential for safety. Hundreds stood in queues every day to get one at Zanu-PF offices, where they were forced to sing songs praising Zanu-PF and denouncing Zapu while they waited.

More selective tactics were used. 5 Brigade took to abducting chosen villagers, holding them in camps where they were beaten, interrogated, and sometimes killed. In conjunction with the CIO, they removed men from buses, trains, and homes. Hundreds disappeared in this manner, never to be seen again.

In 1984 Matabeleland South became the focus of the *Gukurahundi* campaign, following an upsurge of dissident activity there in which several white farmers were killed. Although no more than 200 dissidents were active in the area, the government deployed some 15,000 troops and police, including 5 Brigade, and imposed harsh curfew measures on the civilian population. The area was already suffering from a third year of drought. The local population there, numbering 400,000, was heavily dependent on relief deliveries and food supplies from local stores. In a move that was bound to lead to widespread starvation, the government closed all stores; halted all food deliveries to the area, including drought relief; and enforced a blanket curfew, restricting all movement in and out of curfew zones. Hundreds of thousands of ordinary civilians were quickly reduced to a desperate state. Churchmen pleaded with Mugabe to lift the measures. "Starvation is imminent," they warned. But for two months the measures were kept in place. An officer in 5 Brigade, explaining the army's food policy at a meeting with local Ndebele, said: "First you will eat your chickens, then your goats, then your cattle, then your donkeys. Then you will eat your children and finally you will eat the dissidents." Troops pillaged the land of what food remained and stole cattle, sneering that they were cattle the Ndebele had stolen during raids against the Shona in the nineteenth century. When Chief Ngugana Bango of Sanzukui protested publicly about 5 Brigade's brutality, he was force-marched to their base at Brunapeg Mission, accused of helping dissidents, and beaten so badly that he died. The government claimed he had been killed by dissidents. Many villagers were reduced to eating insects and grass seeds to stay alive. Untold numbers died.

When the Bishop of Bulawayo charged the government with employing a policy of systematic starvation, Mugabe retorted that the bishop was more interested in worshipping Nkomo than God. The security forces, he claimed, had performed "a wonderful duty." Priests should stay out of politics. "It is not when the bishop sneezes that we all catch a cold. No, we are a government and we run our affairs as we see fit.... The fact that bishops speak should not get us running around. What for?"

As well as enforcing the food embargo, 5 Brigade and the CIO rounded up thousands of men, women, and children, even the elderly and infirm, taking them to interrogation centres where they were held sometimes for weeks on end. Army camps such as Bhalagwe became notorious as places of torture and brutality. As many as 2,000 Ndebele were held there at one time, trucked in from all over Matabeleland South. Inmates of Bhalagwe spoke of daily deaths from beating and torture; for survivors, digging graves was a daily chore. Bodies were also taken away by the truckload and dumped in local mine shafts. During a period of four months in 1984, an estimated 8,000 people passed through Bhalagwe. At Stops Police Camp in Bulawayo, detainees were held in "cages" open to all weather and spattered with blood and faeces from previous occupants. The cages were close to interrogation cells, which meant that detainees could hear the screams and moans of those being interrogated day and night.

As the 1985 election approached, Matabeleland was subjected to further violence. Zanu-PF Youth Brigades, modelled on China's Red Guards, were unleashed on the local population, coercing them into buying party cards, forcing thousands onto buses to attend party rallies, and beating anyone who stood in their way. Police watching these events made no effort to intervene. In several urban centres of Matabeleland and in the Midlands, where there was a mixed population of Ndebele and Shona, party youths instigated riots against opposition supporters, stoning and burning homes and in some instances dragging their occupants out onto the streets and beating them to death.

As a prelude to the election, the CIO abducted scores of Zapu officials and councillors—perhaps as many as 400—seizing them from their homes at night. Few were seen or heard from again. In May the Catholic Commission for Justice and Peace managed to lo-cate twenty-five individuals who had disappeared from Silobela, being held in CIO custody in a government prison in Que Que. But this was the only known case of rescue. As well as abductions, the CIO detained hundreds of other Zapu supporters. Addressing an election meeting in Bulawayo, Mugabe issued his own thinly veiled threats to those thinking of voting for Zapu. "Where will we be to-morrow?" he asked. "Is it war or is it peace tomorrow? Let the peo-ple of Matabeleland answer this question."

The violence and abductions had little of the effect Mugabe in-tended. In the 1985 election, with Nkomo back in the country, Zapu won all fifteen parliamentary seats in Matabeleland. Deter-mined to exact revenge, Mugabe appointed as his new police minis-ter Enos Nkala, a man known for his abiding hatred of Nkomo and Zapu. Nkala himself had stood as a Zanu-PF candidate in Mata-beleland South but had received less than 10 percent of the vote and was obliged to find another constituency.

Within a week of Nkala's appointment, the police raided Nkomo's home and arrested his aides and bodyguards. Several hundred Zapu officials were detained, including five members of parliament, eleven councillors on Bulawayo's city council, the mayor, the mayor-elect, the town clerk, and some 200 council employees. Nkala made his intentions clear: "We want to wipe out the Zapu leadership. You've only seen the warning lights. We haven't yet reached full blast. I don't want to hear pleas of mercy. I only want encouragement to deal with this dissident organisation." The organisation, he said, had its roots in Zapu. "My instinct tells me that when you deal with ruthless gangsters, you have to be ruthless. I've locked up a few honourable members [of parliament] and I think they will have a rest for a long time to come before they reappear to continue with their dissident activities."

At a meeting with police commanders in Bulawayo, Nkala outlined the relationship he wanted with the police. According to confidential minutes of the meeting, "the Minister [Nkala] said there would not have been this government without Zanu-PF and you cannot be loyal to the government unless you are also loyal to Zanu-PF."

As well as taking control of the regular police force, Nkala set up a special police intelligence unit known as PISI—Police Internal Security and Intelligence—which he used virtually as his own personal agency. In the Ndebele language, *pisi* meant hyena. PISI gained a reputation for being even more ruthless and brutal than the CIO, acting with complete impunity.

Nkomo attacked the government's use of emergency powers and its blatant disregard for the rule of law:

We accused and condemned the previous white minority government for creating a police state and yet we exceed them when we create a military state. We accused former colonisers who used detention without trial as well as torture and yet do exactly what they did, if not worse. We accused whites of discrimination on grounds of colour and yet we have discriminated on political and ethnic grounds.

Ignoring all protests, Nkala managed stage by stage to grind Zapu down. He banned all Zapu rallies and meetings, then ordered the closure of all Zapu offices. District councils that Zapu controlled were dissolved. "Zanu-PF rules this country," said Nkala, "and anyone who disputes that is a dissident and should be dealt with." There was no longer any pretence that the aim was to crush armed dissidents. It was to crush Zapu, as Mugabe had intended all along.

To avoid further violence and repression, Nkomo capitulated. On December 27, 1987, Mugabe and Nkomo signed a Unity Accord. It merged Zapu and Zanu-PF into a single party, thereafter known as Zanu-PF. Offered an amnesty, the remaining dissidents— 122—handed themselves over to the authorities. An amnesty was also granted to all members of the security forces.

The impact of *Gukurahundi* on Matabeleland was indelible. "This wound is huge and deep," a village headmen said in Lupane in 1996. "The liberation war was painful, but it had a purpose, it was planned, face to face. The war that followed was much worse. It was fearful, unforgettable and unacknowledged."

Mugabe never acknowledged what had happened in Matabeleland or his responsibility for it. All the evidence that was compiled about his government's involvement in mass murder, systematic starvation, torture, and the use of death squads he brushed aside contemptuously. When the human rights organisation Amnesty International provided him with a dossier in 1985, describing how the practice of torture was "widespread" and "persistent," he dismissed it as "a heap of lies," stated that he had no intention of investigating false allegations, and referred to the organisation as "Amnesty Lies International." For years after the conflict had ended, he rejected all appeals for a full inquiry into the Matabeleland atrocities. "If we dig up history, then we wreck the nation...and we tear our people apart into factions, into tribes." When a detailed account of the conflict was published in 1997 as a joint venture by the Catholic Commission for Justice and Peace and the Legal Resources Foundation, using testimony from more than a thousand witnesses, Mugabe retorted that it was merely the work of "mischief makers wearing religious garb." When presented with the findings of two government commissions set up to investigate the violence in Entumbane in 1981 and in Matabeleland South in 1983, he simply suppressed them. His own account of what had happened in Matabeleland in the 1980s he gave in July 2000, at a memorial service for Joshua Nkomo. He admitted that thousands of civilians had been killed but refused to accept any responsibility. "It was an act of madness. We killed each other and destroyed each other's property. It was wrong and both sides were to blame. We have had a difference, a quarrel. We engaged ourselves in a reckless and unprincipled fight."

The burden of blame, however, lies with Mugabe. Determined to achieve a one-party state, he provoked a war against Zapu and its Ndebele and Kalanga supporters, preparing for it well in advance by establishing his own political army, recruited exclusively from Shona supporters and trained by North Korea for special combat duties. The clashes that ensued in the national army precipitated mass desertions of Zipra soldiers fleeing for their lives. A minority banded together as dissidents, but they had no clear goal. "In the 1980s no one was recruited," said one ex-Zipra fighter interviewed by researchers in 1995. "We were forced by the situation. All of us just met in the bush. Each person left on his own, running from death." Another ex-Zipra soldier recalled:

> Some of us who demobilised thought it best to return home because at least you could live in your own home. But little did we know that we were coming to a much worse situation. I did not even have time to spend my demob money before I had to leave to

go to this second war.... Since you were a demobilised Zipra ex-
combatant, they would immediately find you guilty and level you
[kill you] as a dissident.

The dissident campaign that followed, aided and abetted by
South Africa on a minor scale, was brutal and vindictive. Some 600
civilians were murdered, including scores of Zanu-PF members and
some seventy whites, mainly farmers and their relatives. But the
government constantly exaggerated the dissident threat for its own
purposes and persisted in equating support for Zapu as support for
the dissidents. "Zapu inspires dissident activities, inspires banditry,
it inspires lawlessness in the country," Mugabe told parliament in
1985. Yet he never produced any material evidence to support these
claims. Two lengthy treason trials, one in 1982 and one in 1986,
both failed to prove any collusion between Zapu and the dissidents.

Dissident activity nevertheless gave Mugabe just the opportunity he needed to unleash repression across the whole of Matabeleland and to eliminate Zapu in the process. This, essentially, was the
objective of *Gukurahundi* and the specific task given to 5 Brigade
when it was deployed in Matabeleland in January 1983. There was
no disguising the ferocity of its attacks on civilians. In broad daylight, 5 Brigade troops descended on one village after another,
rounding up the entire population, men, women, and children alike,
beating them en masse and executing select groups. The terror they
created was deliberate. It was intended to destroy all traces of political support for Zapu. To this end, over a four-year period, at least
10,000 civilians were murdered, many thousands more were beaten
and tortured, and an entire people were victimised.

The author of this terror was Mugabe. His own speeches licensed it. Only when evidence of the results was presented to him
did he balk at accepting responsibility. The principal instrument of
terror—5 Brigade—was his own creation. Once its function had
been fulfilled, it was disbanded. For Mugabe, none of this was an

aberration. During the Rhodesian war, violence had become his stock-in-trade. Given Smith's intransigence, it was ultimately the only method of gaining majority rule. But once in power Mugabe continued to use violence to achieve his objectives. In the case of Matabeleland, the purpose was to crush opposition from Zapu. But subsequently when other opponents challenged his rule, he resorted to the use of violence time and again. Indeed, he was later to boast that he had "a degree in violence."

# [5]

# THE NEW ELITE

SOON AFTER taking office in 1980, Mugabe's government announced that a 140-acre site in the hills on the western outskirts of Harare would be used to build a national monument commemorating the heroes of the liberation war. Known as Heroes' Acre, the monument includes a giant bronze relief of three guerrillas, two men and a woman, holding weapons. A tomb for the unknown soldier lies between two high walls bearing engraved scenes from the armed struggle. Farther up the hillside stands a forty-metre-high tower carrying the Eternal Flame, which was lit at the 1980 independence celebrations to signify the new spirit of independence. The design of the monument is decidedly foreign. Instead of commissioning Zimbabwean artists, renowned internationally for their sculptures, Mugabe asked North Korea, with its penchant for Stalinist statuary, to undertake the work.

The government stipulated two categories of people who qualified for burial at Heroes' Acre. One group was "national leaders, freedom fighters and the dedicated supporters of the national liberation who participated in or undertook revolutionary activities that contributed directly to the final victory of declaring independence."

The other included "contemporary and future sons and daughters of Zimbabwe of the same calibre as those fallen heroes whose dedication and commitment to the new nation of Zimbabwe will justify their burial at this sacred spot."

Those selected for burial as national heroes were given elaborate funerals and expensive coffins. Their dependants received substantial state benefits. One member of parliament described Heroes' Acre as "a five-star retirement place." It was guarded by the army and remained inaccessible to the public except by special permission.

For those not qualified to join this national elite, the government established a number of local "heroes' acres" in the provinces. Relatives of guerrillas who had died in the war were encouraged to rebury them there but were given no financial assistance or state benefits and were left to pay the expenses themselves. Only Heroes' Acre in Harare was declared a national monument.

Thus, from the start of his administration, even when dealing with an issue as sacred as the liberation struggle, Mugabe developed a caste system, making a clear distinction between the "chefs" who ran the government—a name given to Zanu leaders who had spent the war in exile in Mozambique—and the "povos" or masses they ruled. Despite endless pronouncements about his commitment to transforming Zimbabwe into a socialist society, he never made any moves in that direction, and the gap between the chefs and the povos widened with each passing year. Everyone in government was respectfully referred to as "comrade," but nothing more than lip service was paid to working towards socialist ideals. The rewards of independence went predominantly to members of the elite who displayed loyalty to Mugabe and to Zanu's leadership.

This applied as much to decisions about who qualified for the status of national hero as to other matters. In 1986, General Lookout Masuku, a former Zipra commander, was belatedly released from detention suffering from severe illness and died a few weeks

later. His role in the liberation struggle was well known. As a young
political activist he had participated in the sabotage campaign of the
early 1960s before leaving for military training abroad. As Zipra's
commander he had played a crucial role not only in directing
Zipra's war strategy but in establishing the cease-fire before independence and in the integration exercise afterwards. Arrested in
1982 during the arms cache crisis, he had been tried for treason but
acquitted, then held in detention indefinitely. Nkomo wanted him
to be buried in Heroes' Acre. "If Lookout Masuku is not a hero,
who then is a hero in the country?" he asked. But Mugabe would
have none of it. Masuku was buried in a cemetery in Bulawayo at a
highly emotional funeral attended by 30,000 people but no government representatives. In subsequent years, Mugabe blocked other
prominent figures who had fallen foul of him from receiving due
recognition in Heroes' Acre.

Having demolished his Zapu rivals, Mugabe went on to accumu-
late ever greater powers. Although the unity accord with Zapu had
left him in control of ninety-nine out of a hundred seats in parliament, his goal remained to establish a one-party state giving him
absolute control. He even talked about his intention that Zanu-PF
should "rule forever." In a ceremony on December 30, 1987, accompanied by the refrain *You Are the Only One*, he was declared executive president by parliament, combining the roles of head of
state, head of government, and commander-in-chief of the defence
forces, with powers to dissolve parliament and declare martial law
and the right to run for an unlimited number of terms of office. His
control of appointments to all senior posts in the civil service, the
defence forces, the police, and parastatal organisations gave him a
virtual stranglehold on government machinery and unlimited opportunities to exercise patronage.

Moreover, Mugabe continued to use the totalitarian powers de-
vised by Smith, which he had inherited at independence, to suppress opposition. For ten years after independence, Zimbabwe was

kept in a state of emergency for one six-month period after another, enabling the government to hold anyone in detention without trial and to detain people even when they had been acquitted by the courts. Although the state of emergency was finally lifted in 1990, Mugabe was still able to wield power arbitrarily by using new legislation, the Presidential Powers (Temporary Measures) Act, which allowed him to assume legislative powers in lieu of parliament and to rule, in effect, by decree. Laws like Smith's infamous Law and Order (Maintenance) Act were retained on the statute book.

Mugabe also tightened his grip on the party machine. At a party congress in 1984, in addition to being formally acknowledged as party leader, he was appointed head of a new fifteen-member politburo set up to control government policy and was given the right to choose all its members.

Parliament became less and less relevant. Members were hand-picked by the party and required to toe the party line. After an initial burst of enthusiasm for their new responsibilities, they spent most of their time and energy developing personal and family businesses. Many had little idea of what went on in their constituencies. Some gained more of a reputation for sleeping in the chamber than for debating. Mugabe himself was moved to warn that "the people cannot be fooled for long into accepting do-nothing individuals, or those they judge to be self-aggrandising and seeking to enrich or benefit themselves at their expense." Yet what Mugabe required from parliament was nothing more than total obedience. It soon became clear that the surest way to gain preferment was to praise Mugabe and his ministers unconditionally. Soon after one ambitious MP, Tony Gara, had likened Mugabe to the "second son of God," he was appointed a deputy minister. Mugabe was just as quick to punish those whose loyalty was suspect.

The press, radio, and television were similarly sycophantic. One of Mugabe's first moves after taking office in 1980 was to ensure a compliant press. Using funds provided by Nigeria, the government set up a trust, the Mass Media Trust, to buy out the South African publishing company that had controlled nearly all daily and Sunday newspapers in the country. White editors were summarily sacked and replaced by government appointees. An early sign of how Mugabe intended to deal with the press came when a small weekly newspaper in Umtali (Mutare) reported the arrival of a North Korean military mission in the eastern highlands. In an accompanying comment headlined "Sinister Trend," the white editor questioned the need for such foreign assistance. Two days later she was picked up by CIO officers, driven to Harare to be reprimanded by Mugabe, and then sacked. News coverage became increasingly skewed. Speeches by Mugabe and by cabinet ministers, regardless of their merit, dominated the front pages. Opposition politicians were ignored except for adverse reports. Little was mentioned about the war in Matabeleland other than dissident atrocities. Radio and television were even more slavish in their coverage, serving as crude instruments of party propaganda.

The new elite—ministers, members of parliament, party officials, senior civil servants, and defence and police chiefs—adapted readily to the lifestyle once reserved for privileged whites, moving into spacious houses; driving expensive cars; dining in fashionable restaurants; and buying farms, hotels, and businesses. They enrolled their children in fee-paying schools. Their social routine included sumptuous weddings, lavish funerals, and grand weekend garden parties. Much of their wealth came from backhanders and bribes. Mugabe made clear his disapproval of the "bourgeois" tendencies of the elite and drew up a "leadership code" in 1984 intended to apply to all senior personnel in the upper echelons of the government and the party. The code prohibited them from receiving more than one salary or income from rented property and from owning more than fifty acres of agricultural land, and restricted their ownership of businesses. But no one paid much attention to it. Nor did Mugabe press the issue.

Indeed, in the following year Mugabe gave his approval to the army commander, General Solomon Mujuru, to expand his personal business interests. An influential figure within the Zanu hierarchy, Mujuru had commanded the Zanla unit that opened the Rhodesian war in the northeast. In 1978 he had quelled an internal revolt aimed at toppling Mugabe, thus making him indispensable. As army commander he was alleged to have made a personal fortune from defence procurement contracts, most notably over a deal for Brazilian armoured cars. In 1985 he acquired two adjacent farms in Shamva, a hotel in Bindura, a supermarket chain, and several other properties in the Bindura area, all with Mugabe's blessing. As well as using an official residence in the wealthy suburb of Borrowdale, he lived on a 1,500-acre farm in Ruwa, east of Harare. By the time he resigned from the army in 1992 to devote himself full time to his business affairs, he had become one of the wealthiest individuals in Zimbabwe, all in the space of twelve years.

Zanu-PF endeavoured to build up its own business empire. Its initial venture in 1980 was M&S Syndicate, a holding company for party properties, including some sixty houses in low-density suburbs and six farms. With the help of a group of Asian businessmen, in 1981 it established Zidco Holdings, which focused on import and export businesses and benefited substantially from government and army contracts. The party's printing company, Jongwe Printing and Publishing, produced textbooks and other educational materials for government schools and printed the official parliamentary record. Through Zidco, the party invested in a range of other businesses such as vehicle sales, leaving management in professional hands but ensuring a steady supply of government contracts and import licences. The key figure in the party's business empire was one of Mugabe's most trusted lieutenants, Emmerson Mnangagwa. In 1992 Mnangagwa revealed that Zanu's fixed assets and businesses were worth nearly Z $500 million (US $75 million). But no other financial information was ever disclosed.

The whiff of corruption that emerged from Mugabe's administration and the high living of its chefs caused growing resentment. His promises of a new socialist era appeared increasingly bogus. Although there was a major expansion in education and health services, there was no increase in employment. Tens of thousands of youths left school each year with a reasonable education but no prospect of finding a job. While the elite could afford expensive private education and health facilities, the vast majority of the population faced declining standards in government schools and hospitals, for there were not enough resources available both to fund an increase in services and to maintain them. As inflation rose, wage earners found that the gains they had made in the early years of independence were soon eroded. In rural areas, the land resettlement programme proceeded so slowly that only a tiny fraction of the peasant population benefited; the rest continued to subsist on overcrowded land in tribal reserves.

The plight of thousands of ex-combatants was particularly striking. Many had left school early to join up and possessed neither education nor skills. After demobilisation in 1980, they had been paid monthly stipends for two years but were then left to their own devices. Some set up farming cooperatives, but these soon collapsed. Some scratched a living in communal areas; others roamed the towns searching for work, feeling cheated and disillusioned. Many were destitute. In all, an estimated 30,000 ex-combatants were unemployed. Not until 1988 was their plight raised in parliament. One MP complained that they had been treated "like dogs." Newspapers took up their cause, accusing the government of wilful neglect. "How frustrating and disillusioning it must be to the thousands of ex-combatants in dire straits to observe those with whom they shared the perils of the war of liberation now virtually wallowing in the lap of luxury, while they live in poverty," commented the Bulawayo *Chronicle*. The paper published a letter from an ex-combatant proposing that ministers volunteer "to have their enormously fat salaries cut." The writer asked rhetorically: "Do they need $1,000 per month on housing allowances? Do our socialist 'comrades' need two drivers? Do they need a Benz?" The government promised to set up a special committee to investigate the plight of ex-combatants. But in 1990 the *Chronicle* reported, "Nothing has been heard of that committee since. And nobody seems to care."

Mugabe distanced himself from many of these difficulties, allowing the government to drift on aimlessly. He never developed a clear strategy for economic development other than to pay homage to socialism. When faced with an adverse turn of events, his reaction was to find someone to blame. He was especially quick to believe that the small white community lay behind many problems. During a shortage of maize meal, the staple diet of most Zimbabweans, the government set up a committee that included eight ministers to investigate whether milling companies were responsible for withholding supplies to profit from higher prices. The committee exonerated the milling companies, wholesalers, and retailers, finding that there was no evidence of hoarding; individuals, they decided, accounted for mass purchases, some of which had been smuggled across Zimbabwe's borders to neighbouring countries. Two days later, addressing a Zanu-PF meeting, Mugabe refused to accept the committee's conclusions:

> I will never believe the story that the shortage was caused by so many people now buying mealie meal or that some of the mealie meal was going to Botswana or Mozambique. That is a lie. I know these millers. Their intention is to suck the wealth of the country and destroy the government.... Those whites we defeated are still in control. They own the mines, the factories, commerce. They are the bosses in our country.

Nor did Mugabe permit development initiatives likely to undermine his own control. When Norman Reynolds, formerly the government's chief economist from 1981 to 1986, drew up a financial system for the development of rural areas that involved converting villages into trust companies, his plan was adopted by all fifty-five of the country's district councils at a national conference. When it was subsequently presented to the cabinet, Mugabe simply put the document aside as "not in the party's interest" because "no one need vote for Zanu-PF again." Although more than half of the cabinet had claimed to support the plan, none of them said a word. Reynolds concluded, "Mugabe has always stopped anything that enabled rural people and communities to gain an effective degree of autonomy, particularly financial, as that might reduce his ability to play patron and to use the party and the state to manipulate people and issues."

What interested Mugabe far more than tedious domestic issues was the role he cultivated on the international stage. As a key figure in the Front Line States, the group of southern African countries opposed to the apartheid regime in South Africa, he gained high standing in the international campaign to defeat apartheid. Western governments were anxious to support Zimbabwe in its stand against South Africa and to provide assistance to counter the effects of the Renamo insurgency in Mozambique, which disrupted its trade routes to the coast and spilled across the eastern border. From 1986 to 1989 Mugabe served as chairman of the Non-Aligned Movement, spending much of his time on foreign travel.

Yet for all the foreign glory that Mugabe enjoyed, back home there were growing signs of dissent. In July 1988 parliament suddenly stirred into life when a backbench MP, Byron Hove, presented a well-researched dossier about corruption, mismanagement, and ministerial interference in the national airline, Air Zimbabwe. Others joined the fray, launching into vehement attacks on the government over one issue after another. Among them was Edgar Tekere, Mugabe's outspoken friend from the liberation struggle. Since leaving the government in 1981 Tekere, in between bouts of alcoholism, had pursued a personal crusade against corruption among the new elite, describing them as "a new class of masters" who had "hijacked the revolution" for their own gain. Now he focused his anger on Mugabe's plan for a one-party state. "I fear we are heading towards the creation of a dictatorship," he told a public meeting in Mutare in October 1988. "Democracy in Zimbabwe is in intensive care and the leadership has decayed." He accused cabinet ministers, senior bureaucrats, and security chiefs of stashing away money in Swiss bank accounts "just like the mafia." Four days later, Tekere was expelled from Zanu-PF. Mugabe told the central committee that the party would no longer tolerate "political dissidents and malcontents."

To Mugabe's embarrassment, however, the extent of corruption amongst his own colleagues was exposed as the result of a newspaper investigation. In October 1988 the *Chronicle* revealed details of how a group of politicians, civil servants, and businessmen were involved in a scam to take advantage of a critical shortage of vehicles in the country by buying up cars produced at the state-owned Willowvale factory in Harare, selling them at hugely inflated prices in breach of government price controls and making huge profits for themselves.

The scandal, known as Willowgate, forced Mugabe to set up a commission of inquiry headed by a High Court judge, Wilson Sandura. The commission investigated nine ministers, four MPs, seventeen senior officials including army chiefs, and six businessmen. Among the ministers were two of Mugabe's closest friends, Enos Nkala, then defence minister, and Maurice Nyagumbo, who had been entrusted with special responsibility for administering Zanu-PF's leadership code.

Nkala's first reaction was to threaten to send soldiers to arrest the editor of the *Chronicle*, Geoffrey Nyarota. "Who is little Nyarota?" he asked. He denied any involvement in the car racket. But called before the commission for re-examination, he admitted that he had lied in previous hearings to the commission and re-signed, adding, "I have no apology to make." Another minister, Fred Shava, also admitted to having committed perjury and resigned.

When the commission's report was published in April 1989, three other ministers, including Maurice Nyagumbo, were found to have been guilty and were obliged to resign. They had been seduced by "the evils of the capitalist system," Mugabe explained. All five ministers faced prosecution. For Nyagumbo the humiliation was too great, and he committed suicide. Only one minister, Fred Shava, was subsequently convicted as a result of the investigation. He was given a nine-month sentence for perjury. But after he had spent no more than one night in prison, Mugabe gave him a presidential pardon and ordered that all remaining charges against other ministers should be dropped. "Who amongst us has not lied?" he asked. "Yesterday you were with your girlfriend and you told your wife you were with the president. Should you get nine months for that?"

Thus the entire exercise was turned into a charade. One promi-nent lawyer remarked that the dropping of the perjury charges had given "carte blanche to public officials to lie under oath to judicial bodies." Byron Hove, the MP who had first spoken out against cor-ruption, observed that "there are two laws—one for the leaders and one for the people." To ensure that there were no further press dis-closures, Mugabe ordered the removal of Nyarota from his post as editor of the *Chronicle*.

Public anger at high-level corruption and the relentless decline in living standards gave Tekere an opportunity to make his mark. In April 1989 he launched an opposition party, the Zimbabwe Unity Movement (ZUM), urging his fellow colleagues in Zanu-PF to join and "seek better leadership, clean leadership, for the survival of our country." In the impoverished black suburbs of Harare, Bulawayo, and his home town, Mutare, Tekere gained star status. University students rallied behind him. The white community too found much to admire in his defiant stand against Mugabe.

The first test for Tekere came when he decided to enter ZUM in a parliamentary by-election in Dzivaresekwa, a black suburb of Harare, using the campaign slogan "*murambatsvina*" or "We don't like dirt." In what was to become a familiar routine for opposition movements, ZUM was harassed at every turn. The police refused to give Tekere permission to hold a single rally in Harare; two of his officials were detained for a week; fifteen supporters were held on suspicion of subversion; and the press refused to accept any advertisements and mounted a propaganda campaign in favour of the government. Yet ZUM, with no office, no manifesto, and no proper organisation and undermined by vote-rigging, still gained 30 percent of the vote.

The focal point of opposition moved to the university. When students were forcibly prevented by police from holding a demonstration against corruption, two student leaders issued a statement accusing the government of practising "state terrorism" comparable to the methods used by the apartheid regime in South Africa. The government's response was to send fully armed police to arrest the student leaders, invoking Rhodesian emergency powers legislation. In the ensuing violence, police fired tear-gas grenades into residential halls, assaulted students, and set up a makeshift detention camp opposite the main gate of the university. Although examinations were due to be held in two weeks' time, the vice-chancellor decided to order the closure of the university.

The brutal handling of student protest drew expressions of shock from both church leaders and the trade union movement. Never in its thirty-two-year history had the university been closed before or witnessed such violence. The events at the university, said Morgan Tsvangirai, secretary-general of the Zimbabwe Congress of Trade Unions (ZCTU), were "a clear manifestation of rising state repression." In a wide-ranging attack on government policies, he accused Mugabe of trying to suppress public discontent over soaring prices, unemployment, and destitution through "the naked use of brute state force and the suppression of individual rights."

LEFT: One of the few photographs of Robert Mugabe in combat uniform. *(Sunday Times Archives)*

BELOW: Robert Mugabe and Joshua Nkomo *(right and second from right)* were still closely allied at the time of the signing of the cease-fire and constitutional agreement at Lancaster House in London on 21 December 1979. Also present were *(from right)* Britain's Lord Gilmour, Foreign Secretary Lord Carrington and Bishop Abel Muzorewa. *(Sunday Times Archives)*

RIGHT: Mugabe and British foreign secretary Lord Carrington meet in London in 1980. *(Sunday Times Archives)*

BELOW: Zanu-PF supporters take over the streets of Harare in the run-up to the first fully democratic election in Rhodesia. *(Sunday Times Archives)*

Rhodesian Front leader Ian Smith reflects on the results of the country's first democratic election on 27 and 28 February 1980.
*(Sunday Times Archives)*

Lord Soames on his return to Britain, after serving as governor until the elections in 1980.
*(Sunday Times Archives)*

LEFT: Joshua Nkomo, leader of the Zimbabwe African People's Union, pictured in 1976. *(Sunday Times Archives)*

BELOW: Mugabe at a rally in Norton in 1982, at which he accused the Patriotic Front member Zapu of plotting against his Zanu-PF party. By the end of that year the newly-formed 5th Brigade, specially trained by North Koreans to deal with internal dissidents, began its assault on Mugabe opponents. *(Sunday Times Archives)*

LEFT: Sally, Mugabe's first wife, born in Ghana, was a popular figure in her own right. When she died in January 1992, Mugabe lost his closest friend and the only person who was able to moderate his mood swings.
*(Sunday Times Archives)*

BELOW: Southern African leaders at a trade and investment summit in Gaberone in 1997. *(From left)* Robert Mugabe, Mozambique's president Joaquim Chissano, Namibian prime minister Hage Geingob and Gauteng premier Tokyo Sexwale.
*(Sunday Times/ Lori Waselchuk)*

Mugabe arrives at the National Economic Consultative Forum in 1998.
*(Sunday Times/Nicky de Blois)*

Mugabe and his second wife Grace, (formerly a secretary in his office, who became known for her lavish style of living), at the opening of the Kingdom Hotel in Victoria Falls in 1999.
*(Sunday Times)*

LEFT: Mugabe and President Nelson Mandela at the Union Buildings in 1995. *(Sunday Times/John Hrusa)*

BELOW: Cartoon published in *Sunday Times*, Johannesburg on 18 February 2001.

TOP: Chitungwiza township outside Harare on 23 January 1998, after a mob had attacked and burned a police vehicle during riots in protest against food price rises.
(Sunday Times/Nicky de Blois)

BOTTOM: As demonstrations against the government increased in the late 1990s, ove government food price control and corrupti riot police became a familiar sight in Harar
(Sunday Times Archives)

Mugabe's retaliation was swift. Tsvangirai was arrested by CIO officers, taken from his home barefoot and handcuffed, and then held for five days, denied access to lawyers. The High Court intervened, decided that the reasons given for his arrest were unsatisfactory, and ordered his immediate release. He was nominally released but was re-arrested and detained almost immediately on allegations that he was a South African spy and agent provocateur. When the High Court ruled again that his detention was unlawful, he was released only to be re-detained almost immediately. For more than a month he was held in prison before finally being set free.

Student leaders were dealt with in similar fashion. All fifteen members of the Students Representative Council were held on charges of publishing and possessing a subversive document. When they applied for bail, the minister of home affairs issued a ministerial certificate barring the granting of bail on the grounds that it would prejudice the administration of justice. Only when the High Court threw out the certificate were they released.

The student protest and the ensuing events demonstrated how ruthless Mugabe was prepared to be in suppressing any sign of opposition. All the hallmarks of his presidency were there to be seen: police violence and intimidation, assaults, arbitrary arrests, false accusations and charges, and contempt for the courts. There was no pretence that security issues were at stake, as there had been in the case of Matabeleland. This was just repression of dissent against a corrupt elite.

In the weeks before the 1990 elections Mugabe awarded himself further powers over parliament. The number of seats was increased to 150, but only 120 were to be contested directly on the common voters' roll. Twenty were to be appointments made by the president himself, and ten more were to be customary chiefs elected by the Council of Chiefs, in effect, appointments that Mugabe also controlled. The change meant that even if an opposition party gained a majority of seats in a parliamentary election, it would not necessarily obtain enough seats to form a government. Mugabe could use his own appointees to block it. Zanu-PF needed only forty-six seats to form a majority in parliament; the opposition needed seventy-six seats.

Moreover, Mugabe ensured that Zanu-PF had access to state funding. As a result of legislation passed in 1986, the Political Parties (Finance) Act, parties holding more than fifteen seats in parliament were entitled to financial support. In effect, the state was financing Zanu-PF's election campaign, while opposition parties were left floundering.

The 1990 elections were of more than usual significance. Mugabe intended to use them as a stepping stone to a one-party state, and Tekere was determined to stop him. Tekere's campaign was handicapped from the start. Not only did he suffer from a reputation as a hothead with alcoholic tendencies, but he decided to team up with others of dubious distinction. These included members of the all-white Conservative Alliance of Zimbabwe, the direct descendants of Ian Smith's Rhodesian Front.

One of Tekere's most prominent allies was Patrick Kombayi, a former leading figure in Zanu-PF who, as mayor of Gweru, the third largest town in Zimbabwe, had established a virtual dictatorship there. No sooner had he taken office than he ordered a mayoral car—where there had previously been none—with instructions that it should be either a Rolls Royce or Mercedes, declaring simultaneously a 50 percent increase in local taxes. To illustrate his style of leadership, he commissioned a photograph of himself clenching an iron bar with his teeth, asking the local newspaper to publish it with the caption: "I have teeth. I can bite." He announced that henceforth he intended personally to vet the renewal of all traders' licences. Businessmen, both black and white, were ordered to a meeting where they were harangued by the mayor and his committee. He put more than a hundred of his supporters on the town payroll as a personal police force and directed council contracts towards his own businesses. He summoned to his office a lawyer representing a theatre group that was in dispute with the council and assaulted him, breaking his nose and bruising his face, then threw him out with the words: "Go, see what your law and your courts can do now." His notoriety became sufficiently serious for Zanu-PF to suspend him from office and expel him from the party. But he remained a popular figure in Gweru, and Tekere readily recruited him as a ZUM candidate.

Mugabe brought to the election campaign his customary mix of blandishments and threats. He warned public sector employees that they would be sacked if they voted for ZUM, and he licensed party thugs to take action against opponents. "We are saddened that there are others who want to divide us," he said. "But people must not listen to small, petty little ants which we can crush." He warned whites contemplating voting for ZUM: "That Tekere nonsense should stop. If the whites in Zimbabwe want to rear their ugly terrorist and racist head by collaborating with ZUM, we will chop that head off." The same threats of violence were used by Zanu-PF in its campaign advertisements. One television advertisement, watched by many viewers with astonishment and disbelief, featured the screech of tyres and the crushing of glass and metal in a car accident, followed by a voice warning coldly: "This is one way to die. Another is to vote ZUM. Don't commit suicide, vote Zanu-PF and live." Another advertisement showed a coffin being lowered into a grave followed by the warning: "AIDS kills. So does ZUM. Vote Zanu-PF." A Zanu-PF candidate told his constituents that the party would "go back to war if it loses the election."

The campaign followed a predictable course. While government and army vehicles were used to ferry people to Zanu-PF rallies, ZUM found it difficult to hold rallies at all. The media gave saturation coverage to Zanu-PF but little to ZUM. In Harare's Mufakose township, gangs of Zanu-PF youths armed with bricks and hosepipes roamed the streets, clashing with anyone suspected of supporting ZUM or other opposition parties. Similar intimidation occurred in other urban areas. But the worst violence erupted in Gweru. It was also the scene of blatant manipulation.

Gweru was divided into three constituencies. In Gweru Central there was a fierce contest between Patrick Kombayi and Simon Muzenda, one of Mugabe's two vice-presidents. In the neighbouring Gweru South constituency, Zanu-PF had a clear lead, with strong support. On March 24, only four days before the start of the election, a presidential proclamation was issued in the name of the Delimitation Commission, which was responsible for defining constituency boundaries, making alterations to Gweru's boundaries. The Mkoba suburb, where Kombayi was hugely popular, was excised from Gweru Central and transferred to Gweru South, effectively depriving him of his strongest base of support and giving the edge to Muzenda.

On that same day a gang of Zanu-PF youths gathered outside Kombayi's Mini-Mart shop in Ridgemont, singing Zanu songs, including "Kombayi must die." They stoned windows, looted the shop, broke open the safe, set fire to the building, and fired shots at ZUM supporters. Alerted to the trouble, Kombayi arrived on the scene and organised a truck to take the wounded to hospital, deciding that he would follow in his own car. On its way to hospital the truck was waved down by armed CIO agents, who opened fire, hitting the driver in the stomach. The truck veered off the road. Uniformed police, armed CIO agents, and Zanu-PF supporters rushed towards it. The vehicle was set on fire. Following behind, Kombayi stopped at the scene, but before he could open the car door CIO officers, in the presence of the uniformed police, fired a volley of shots into the car. Six bullets hit Kombayi, shattering his left leg, injuring his right leg, and passing through his stomach. Bleeding heavily, Kombayi put his hand through the window, shouting, "Okay, stop, you have killed me." He opened the door and fell onto the road.

Mugabe won a convincing victory in the 1990 elections. In the parliamentary contest, Zanu-PF gained 116 of 119 seats; ZUM gained only two. In the presidential contest, Mugabe obtained nearly 80 percent of the vote, leaving Tekere trailing with 16 percent. But the two parliamentary seats that ZUM won effectively meant the end of Mugabe's dream for a one-party state.

Kombayi failed to win his seat in Gweru, and he remained a cripple for life. Two men, a senior CIO officer and a Zanu-PF youth leader, were subsequently convicted of attempted murder. But within hours of the Supreme Court dismissing their appeal against conviction, Mugabe gave them a presidential pardon and they were set free. He also pardoned groups of Zanu-PF youths convicted of election violence.

"We have a president who does not believe in the rule of law and who disregards the tenancy upon which the rule of law is built," said Enoch Dumbutshena, a former chief justice. "To ordinary people, it's more frightening because it means the president has given a licence to members of Zanu-PF and CIO to kill those who are not members of their party in full knowledge that the president will pardon them."

# [6]

# FAMILY AFFAIRS

IN TEN YEARS in office, Mugabe had become an increasingly re-mote and authoritarian figure. His official residences in Harare were heavily fortified. He travelled only in large motorcades sur-rounded by retinues of armed bodyguards with screaming sirens heard for miles around. He openly admired dictators such as Nico-lae Ceausescu of Romania, praising him the day before he was over-thrown by popular revolution. Party advertisements in newspapers paid homage to Mugabe as "our Consistent and Authentic Leader," emulating the style of communist personality cults. He lectured endlessly on the merits of communism, insisting that Zimbabwe's future was "better guaranteed under one single, monolithic and gi-gantic political party." As president, he was no longer required to attend parliament and answer questions on government policy, and his ministers were similarly able to evade policy issues by claiming they were the prerogative of the president. He created a February 21 youth movement, named after his birthday, ostensibly to help needy youths acquire leadership skills but used principally to cele-brate his birthday. His photograph hung on the wall of every gov-ernment office.

His wife, Sally, was included in the glorification. Mugabe instructed the media to refer to her as "Amai," meaning "mother of the nation." He appointed her head of the Zanu-PF Women's League and gave her a place on the politburo, prompting Tekere to describe Mugabe's rule as a "bedroom-based personal dictatorship." Sally used her position to profit from business dealings. But she also acted at crucial times as an anchor in reality for Mugabe. A formidable woman in her own right, she managed to curb some of the wilder excesses of his anger and ambition. She also won much respect and popularity for her work with children's organisations and other charities.

Both were deeply affected by the loss of their children during Rhodesian days. It was, said Sally, "the saddest thing that happened to us." Sally suffered from a kidney ailment that doctors predicted would end her life prematurely. "I knew the life of my first wife was going to be short," said Mugabe in a television interview in 1998, "so I knew how to prepare for life after her."

In 1987, at the age of sixty-three, Mugabe embarked on an affair with a secretary in his office, Grace Marufu, who was forty years younger than he. "I wanted children, and this is how I thought I could get them," he explained. Sally was aware of the arrangement. Mugabe remarked, "I knew what I was doing and my wife knew. She might not have liked it, but she knew about it." The affair was complicated by the fact that Grace was already married, with a son. Their liaison was conducted in total secrecy. Their first child was born in 1988, a daughter named Bona, after Mugabe's mother, followed two years later by a son named Robert.

When Sally died in January 1992, Mugabe lost not only a trusted companion who had stood by him through years of imprisonment and revolutionary warfare but a friend able to moderate his moods. He possessed no other close friends. Those colleagues close to him in the past had fallen away: Edgar Tekere had become his fiercest critic, Enos Nkala had been disgraced by the Willowgate scandal and left the government, and Maurice Nyagumbo had committed suicide. Asked about his lack of close friends in 1998, Mugabe replied: "I avoid, you know, a relationship that is far, far too close, with one or two individuals. Why should that happen?"

In the wake of the 1990 election, Mugabe reluctantly agreed to "postpone" his plans for a one-party state. Within the Zanu-PF hierarchy, there had been growing misgivings about its merits. The downfall of communist dictatorships in eastern Europe, including Ceaucescu's regime in Romania, had made the idea seem obsolete. Western aid donors, moreover, began to demand political reform in favour of multiparty systems as the price for their support. Zimbabwe's neighbour, Mozambique, once a staunch Marxist ally, announced in 1990 its intention to set up a multiparty system. In South Africa the release of Nelson Mandela from prison and the lifting of the ban on the African National Congress opened the prospect of a more democratic era there. Leading figures in Zanu-PF were keen to improve Zimbabwe's standing with foreign investors and donors. But Mugabe was not easily persuaded. According to Jonathan Moyo, a prominent political commentator, he had to be dragged "kicking and screaming" from his goal. In 1991 Zanu-PF formally discarded all references in its constitution to "Marxism-Leninism" and "scientific socialism." Mugabe still insisted that "socialism remains our sworn ideology." But his claim was as meaningless in the 1990s as it had been in the 1980s.

The cavalcade of greed and corruption gathered new momentum. Fraud, forgery, theft, and embezzlement in government departments became endemic. The chairman of parliament's public accounts committee, Alois Mangwende, reported in 1993 that "corruption has become so pervasive and civil servants so venal and rapacious" that virtually no service was provided without "kickbacks and cuts." No one could get papers or certificates without payment.

Hardly a waste basket was bought by the government without someone wanting some kind of kickback: "Goods worth millions are bought from dubious agents with the ultimate idea of getting kickbacks." In one case, a civil servant imported enough pencils to meet the needs of the country for fifty years, earning a handsome commission. Government buyers placed orders with rogue traders quoting inflated prices to make a killing: "There is a tendency for suppliers to overcharge and civil servants to overpay them and share the spoils later without a tinge of guilt," Mangwende complained. Senior officials invented expenses, ministers refused to account for travel allowances, police commissioners were equally corrupt.

The toll on state-owned enterprises, all staffed by Zanu-PF appointees, was especially severe. One by one the national airline, the railways, the National Oil Company, the Grain Marketing Board, the Zimbabwe Electricity Supply Authority, the Posts and Telecommunications Corporation, the National Social Security Authority, and the District Development Fund were all hit by gross mismanagement, rampant graft, and outright theft. "The rate at which Government and its parastatals, financial institutions and industrial concerns are being defrauded of millions of dollars is indeed alarming," the minister of home affairs admitted in July 1993. Yet year after year the looting continued uninterrupted, bringing them ever closer to bankruptcy.

Ministers, senior officials, and their business associates meanwhile muscled in on some of the government's more lucrative contracts. When bids were invited for a new US $80 million airport terminal in Harare in 1993, several international companies submitted designs. The contract was awarded by the Tender Board to France's Aéroports de Paris. But the president's nephew, Leo Mugabe, intervened on behalf of a little-known Cyprus firm, Air Harbour Technologies (AHT), asking the government to reopen the bidding process. AHT, owned by Hani Yamani, son of a Saudi oil minister, had submitted a design that was considered defective, cost more than any other bid, and was ranked only fourth; furthermore, a Transport Ministry report judged AHT to lack sufficient experience with such projects. Nevertheless, at Leo Mugabe's behest, ministers rejected the Tender Board's decision and ordered the tender process to be reopened.

When the contract for the design and implementation of the new airport building was subsequently awarded to AHT, there were immediate accusations that ministers had accepted bribes to rig the bid. Yamani denied it at the time, but after falling out with his business associates, he wrote a seven-page letter to Mugabe in July 1999, claiming that he had paid US $3 million to ministers, government officials, and business partners to win the contract. Among the payments he listed were US $190,000 to Leo Mugabe, the son of Mugabe's sister, Sabina, and a total of US $350,000 to four government ministers, including the minister of transport and the ubiquitous Emmerson Mnangagwa. He also paid US $20,000 to Zidco, the Zanu-PF trading company, part of a US $1 million contribution he said he had allocated for a new private residence for Mugabe.

Yamani portrayed himself as the victim of a malicious conspiracy. "I have personally been threatened with physical harm if I visit Zimbabwe again, where I have a beautiful house and many dear friends.... I am a victim of plotters who derive all power from you, but who deal for their personal ambitions and agenda." Mugabe admitted publicly that he knew that his ministers were corrupt. "I know that they [some companies] are buying you for tenders and that some of you are accepting huge bribes," he said in July 1999. But he let the corruption continue nevertheless. It was part of his system of patronage and control.

The rewards for a select number of businessmen who fed off the system were considerable. Among the most prominent was a group sometimes referred to as the Zezuru mafia, who came from Mugabe's Zezuru branch of the Shona people. Leo Mugabe was a leading member. As well as his cut in the airport contract, Leo's companies won numerous government tenders, including a US $7 million contract to build a sewage plant for Harare. Another leading member was Phillip Chiyangwa, who boasted about how rich he had become through his links with Zanu-PF. Born in Mugabe's home district of Zvimba, he started out as an entrepreneur in the early 1980s, promoting boxing and music groups, and he also ran a secretarial and accountancy agency. By the 1990s he had become a multi-millionaire, owning a mansion and tourist complex in Zvimba, a private jet, and a range of manufacturing and engineering companies.

Any businessman who tried to operate outside the system encountered severe difficulties. The case of Strive Masiyiwa provides a stark illustration. One of the most talented entrepreneurs that Zimbabwe ever produced, Masiyiwa grew up in exile, qualified as a telecommunications engineer in Britain, and returned home at independence in 1980, working first for the state-owned Posts and Telecommunications Corporation (PTC), then founding his own electrical engineering firm. In 1990 he won a loan from the International Finance Corporation, a World Bank affiliate, to expand his business, the first black Zimbabwean to do so.

Eager to encourage other black Zimbabweans in business, Masiyiwa helped to establish the Indigenous Business Development Centre (IBDC), gaining support from both Western donors and white business interests. But the success of IBDC soon attracted the attention of the Zanu-PF business mafia, who wanted to use it for their own ends, and Masiyiwa resigned. "This country is full of 'commission agents' who try to pass themselves off as businessmen and industrialists," he said. "They produce nothing, they are well-connected politically. When any big government contract comes up, these guys line up to get a cut of the action. I don't like commission agents and I don't pay bribes."

In 1993 Masiyiwa decided to set up a cellular network in Zimbabwe. The existing telephone service provided by the PTC was abysmal. Phone lines were frequently out of order for weeks on end; waiting times for new phones stretched indefinitely. The potential seemed promising. Masiyiwa first approached the PTC suggesting a joint venture, but he was told that there was no demand for mobile telephones in Zimbabwe. He therefore decided to set out on his own, launching a company called Econet.

The government tried to block his efforts at every turn. It claimed that only the PTC had the right to operate a phone system. For more than two years Masiyiwa fought a legal battle, vilified by ministers. "My crime was not to play the commission agent game. Overnight I became a traitor. They called me a CIA agent, a South African agent. My firm lost all its government contracts." But eventually he was vindicated by a special Constitutional Court, which ruled in December 1995 that the PTC's monopoly violated the constitutional right to free speech.

No sooner had Masiyiwa started setting up base stations around Harare than Mugabe himself intervened, issuing a presidential decree that required prospective cellular phone operators to abide by a new set of complex regulations and to seek government approval. While Masiyiwa was forced into further delay, the PTC decided to launch its own plans for a cellular network and started the first cellular service in September 1996. Still facing obstruction, Masiyiwa was obliged to resort once more to legal action. In December 1996 the Supreme Court ordered the information minister, Joyce Mujuru, to grant Econet an operating licence.

By this time, however, another group called Telcel had decided to make a bid to operate a second network. Owned by a Zairean and an American, Telcel had acquired influential local partners, including Leo Mugabe, Phillip Chiyangwa, and James Makamba, a close business associate of Solomon Mujuru, the wealthy former army commander and husband of the minister Joyce Mujuru.

The outcome was predictable. In March 1997 the government's Tender Board awarded the contract for the second network to Telcel. No one was in any doubt about the corruption involved. The independent weekly *Financial Gazette* described the tender system as nothing more than "a vehicle for the powerful in Zimbabwe's society to enrich themselves and their cronies."

Hoping to finish off Masiyiwa, the government announced that there would be no third licence. Joyce Mujuru ordered Masiyiwa to sell his equipment or face confiscation. If he persisted in defying the government, she said, the police or the CIO might be called on to arrest him on security grounds for illegally possessing it. She claimed that Masiyiwa was insolvent and incapable of running a cellular business.

Determined to persevere, Masiyiwa sued for the right to see details of Telcel's bid. As he had expected, it met few of the tender's specifications. Once more he returned to the courts. In December 1997 the entire tender procedure was nullified by Judge President Wilson Sandura. He cited "unforgivable flaws" in the adjudication of the tender and awarded the network licence to Econet.

Thwarted by the courts, Leo Mugabe and his friends still wanted a slice of the action. They turned to the president for support, suggesting they should be given a minority interest—25 percent—of Econet's shares. But Masiyiwa would have none of it. Within a week of starting his cellular operations in July 1998, Econet had gained 10,000 customers; within two months, it had taken nearly half of the market; at the end of a year, it had 70,000 customers. Masiyiwa went on to become a highly successful international entrepreneur.

The elite's favourite businessman was Roger Boka, a Harare tycoon who launched his own bank and handed out millions in loans to prominent politicians and businessmen. What gave him particular status was the relish with which he lambasted the white business community. He filled hundreds of pages in the local press with advertisements vilifying white businessmen, accusing them of conspiring to prevent blacks from gaining economic power. He liked to be known as "the godfather of the indigenisation crusade," blazing a trail to capture the bastions of white-controlled business.

His business origins were humble. In the 1970s he moved from job to job, working as an insurance clerk, a stock controller, and a marketing manager. Then in the early 1980s he won a government contract to supply stationery and books to schools throughout the country. He branched out into gold mining, setting up a joint venture with a Russian company, Siberian Associates.

In 1995, against the advice of its own banking regulators, the government awarded Boka a banking licence and helped to get his United Merchant Bank off the ground, channelling government business his way, including a deal to issue debt on behalf of the state-owned Cold Storage Company. Boka's style became increasingly flamboyant. He often moved around in a motorcade and liked to distribute $100 notes liberally.

Boka then set his sights on building what he described as the biggest tobacco auction floors in the world, once the preserve of white business. The floors opened in 1997, and in March 1998 Boka offered 40 percent of the shares to the public. His business associates hailed him as "an economic hero." The "Boka Tobacco Revolution," as it was called, was said to mark "the Genesis of Zimbabwe's economic jihad."

Six weeks later, his empire collapsed overnight. In April 1998 the United Merchant Bank had its licence revoked after it was discovered that the bank could no longer meet depositors' claims and that its liquidity ratio was too low to meet debt obligations and other liabilities. Upon investigation, Boka was found to have issued fraudulent Cold Storage Company bills to the value of Z $945 million (about US $50 million). He had also siphoned off nearly US $21 million of depositors' funds to his offshore accounts. The scale of the fraud threatened to cause the collapse of other financial institutions, which faced huge losses, forcing the government to step in with a rescue package.

The central bank governor, Leonard Tsumba, was scathing in his indictment of what had happened and censured the government for issuing Boka a licence in the first place: "UMB was grossly mismanaged and was operated in total disregard of laws, rules and regulations. Funds were lost through poor lending, insider loans, externalisation of funds and gross mismanagement." The bank was insolvent to the tune of Z $2.6 billion, said Tsumba. Boka had ignored all corporate governance principles, never called meetings of UMB's board of directors, and granted substantial loans to eleven other companies he controlled. Tsumba's conclusion was that Boka should be prosecuted for fraud, corruption, and money laundering.

Boka was declared a "specified person" under the Prevention of Corruption Act, opening the way for an investigation into his business affairs. He claimed he was owed $2.8 billion, the bulk of it by government ministers, politicians, parastatal companies, and local businessmen. With the connivance of government officials, in June 1998 Boka fled to the United States, where he owned a mansion in Atlanta, Georgia. He returned secretly to Harare in November and stayed for six weeks but was allowed to leave for the United States again. He died in February 1999 without ever facing prosecution.

Few people within Zanu-PF were prepared to take a stand against the juggernaut of power and corruption over which Mugabe presided. The consequences would be ruin or possibly death. But a brave attempt was made during the 1990s by a young Zanu loyalist with impeccable credentials.

Margaret Dongo had joined the Zanu war effort at the age of fifteen, crossing into Mozambique in 1975, the same year as Mugabe, and serving there as a medical assistant. After independence she worked for the CIO but resigned in 1989 to stand in the 1990 elections. She was a member of the central committee, a founding member of the War Veterans Association, and an active member of the Women's League.

Dongo became increasingly disillusioned with the rampant corruption within the government. In parliament she drew attention to the plight of war veterans living in abject poverty and accused senior government officials of enriching themselves with funds intended for ex-combatants. She also criticised older politicians who clung to power, a reference aimed at Mugabe and his two elderly vice-presidents. "I would have died for Mugabe," she said. "But once they got their farms, houses and limos they forgot about the people who put them there."

Zanu-PF leaders resolved to get rid of her but discovered that she had built up solid support in her constituency in Harare and could not be dislodged easily. Party chefs threw their weight behind an alternative candidate. Undaunted, Dongo announced that she would stand as an independent candidate, while remaining a loyal party member. "I am not fighting to get back into parliament," she said. "I am trying to pave a way for democracy." Expelled from the party, she protested that Zanu-PF had "deviated from its course" and was "now being run like a private company."

In the 1995 elections Zanu-PF, boosted by huge state subsidies under the Political Parties (Finance) Act and cheered on by the state-controlled media, predictably won another sweeping victory, taking 118 of 120 elected seats, nearly half of which were uncontested. But it had no answers to the country's growing impoverishment, and the promises of greater prosperity it had made during the campaign were worthless. As the political commentator Jonathan Moyo wrote in the *Financial Gazette* on the eve of the election: "Zanu-PF has no political philosophy beyond the desire of its leadership to stay in power by hook or by crook."

The official results showed that Margaret Dongo had lost in her bid to win the Harare South constituency by 1,097 votes. But she was convinced that the vote had been rigged. The day after the announcement of the results, she publicly asked the registrar-general to investigate the matter. But neither the registrar-general nor the Electoral Supervisory Commission was prepared to intervene. So Dongo decided to appeal to the High Court.

In her application Dongo challenged not only the results of the vote for her own constituency but the entire basis on which the electoral process was managed. Under the Electoral Act, the president had the sole right to appoint the registrar-general and all members of the Electoral Supervisory Commission, the Election Directorate, and the Delimitation Commission. There was no independent body to monitor the election. The registrar-general, in particular, wielded enormous power over the process. "In terms of the Act, the power to conduct an election is vested in the [registrar-general] who is basically not answerable to anyone except his executive masters," Dongo asserted in her affidavit. "The [Electoral] Act and the election procedures as defined in the Constitution are defective and open to manipulation, particularly by a capricious and undemocratic Government such as the current one."

The registrar-general, Tobaiwa Mudede, who had held office since 1980, was already a controversial figure. Opposition parties and civic groups had repeatedly accused him of conducting elections in a partisan manner favouring Zanu-PF and of obstructing their own endeavours. His management of the voters' roll had been criticised by the Electoral Supervisory Commission time and again. He himself admitted the roll was "in a shambles." An independent inquiry into the state of the voters' roll in Harare South, carried out after the 1995 election, showed that of a total of 33,261 voters' names listed on the roll, about 13,600—some 41 percent—were not genuine. Other constituencies were known to face the same problem. The opportunities for electoral fraud were legion.

In the case of Harare South, the High Court found that the number of ballot papers in the ballot boxes exceeded the number of voters by 1,025, and they nullified the result. The judge politely attributed the discrepancy to "a failure on the part of the Registrar-General to ensure that the principles of the Electoral Act were complied with." But others were not so charitable. John Makumbe, a university lecturer who made a special study of the 1995 election, wrote, "Whatever the Judge's reasons for sparing the Registrar-

General, an outsider is more inclined to believe that there had been a deliberate attempt to rig the election against Margaret Dongo, including by way of stuffing the ballot box." He concluded, "It is likely that the ruling party might have won elections in many other constituencies through the deliberate and fraudulent manipulation of the electoral process."

Faced with a by-election, party chefs let loose a ferocious campaign against Dongo, trying to destroy her reputation and credibility. Party thugs broke up her rallies; the state-controlled press vilified her. But Dongo persevered, and in November 1995 she duly won Harare South. It was a small victory against the monstrous machine that Mugabe had created. Yet it was to provide a new voice willing to speak out on behalf of deprived groups such as the war veterans.

For three years after Sally's death, Mugabe's liaison with Grace Marufu and the birth of their two children were kept secret from the public. Then, in April 1995, an independent monthly magazine, *Horizon*, after interviewing Grace's father and other family members, reported that Mugabe had fathered two children and subsequently married Grace in a traditional African ceremony, paying the customary *lobola*, or bride price. The article was accompanied by a picture of seven-year-old Bona attending a convent school with her bag clearly marked "Mugabe." The article added that Mugabe intended to announce plans for a legal marriage shortly after the elections were over. Another journal, the *Financial Gazette*, embellished the story by claiming that Mugabe had in fact already married Grace during the Easter holiday at a civil wedding ceremony witnessed by a High Court judge and a cabinet minister.

Mugabe was infuriated that his private affairs had been aired in this manner. The police arrested the publisher of the *Financial Gazette* and two editors at their homes and held them for questioning over the weekend. Mugabe, the judge, and the cabinet minister all denied the report. But the *Financial Gazette* twice printed statements standing by its story, implying that the officials were lying. As a result the three journalists were subsequently prosecuted for criminal defamation, found guilty, and fined.

Far from opting for a secret wedding, Mugabe eventually decided to stage what the state-controlled press described as "the wedding of the century." He wanted it to be performed by the head of the Catholic Church, Archbishop Patrick Chakaipa, to give it respectability and status. Mugabe's insistence on this matter split the Catholic community. It was not just Mugabe's adulterous relationship with Grace that caused offence, or the fact that their two children had been born out of wedlock; there were doubts about whether Grace had been baptised and whether the Church should dignify the affair with a full Catholic ceremony. By sanctioning Mugabe's marriage in those circumstances, the Church would clearly be seen to be confused about its own morality; its prophetic role would be undermined. Many priests recognised, moreover, that Mugabe no longer had any regard for the Catholic Church but was merely using it for his own purposes. Under pressure from Mugabe, however, Chakaipa wilted and agreed to officiate.

The wedding, on August 17, 1996, in the tiny church at Kutama Mission, was indeed the most lavish occasion that Zimbabwe had ever witnessed. Twelve thousand people were invited. The best man was Joachim Chissano, the president of Mozambique. But by far the biggest cheers were for Nelson Mandela, then president of South Africa, who, to Mugabe's intense irritation, remained the star of the show. The two Mugabe children, Bona and Robert, were included in the official photographs; a third was soon under way.

As Mugabe's wife, Grace soon gained a reputation for being interested in little other than shopping, clothes, and jewellery. She was a shallow woman, possessing none of Sally's vivaciousness or her real concern for charitable causes. But Mugabe delighted in taking her on official trips around the world, commandeering the national airline whenever necessary, and indulging her love of luxury.

As the public soon discovered, Grace was also corrupt. She acquired ten acres of land in the affluent suburb of Borrowdale on which to build a mansion, paying the government Z $78,206 for the site when government evaluators valued it at Z $570,000. She then took advantage of an illegal housing scheme hatched by officials in the Ministry of Public Construction and National Housing to build houses for VIP beneficiaries, including cabinet ministers, senior civil servants, and defence and police chiefs. The scheme was later declared by a High Court judge to be both corrupt and illegal, but it enabled Grace to build her mansion at an estimated cost of Z $6 million and then advertise it for sale for Z $25 million. It was eventually sold to the Libyan government for Z $35 million.

With three children and a young, ambitious wife on his hands, Mugabe decided it was time for him to build a grand family mansion of his own in Harare. He chose a twenty-five-acre site in Borrowdale, two miles from the house Grace had built, and commissioned architects to design a huge, three-story residence. Grace busied herself with the internal décor, sparing no expense.

# [7]

# THE LAND ISSUE

No other group received such favourable attention from Mugabe when he gained power in 1980 as white farmers. Their role was regarded as crucial to the economic welfare of Zimbabwe. They accounted for three-quarters of the output of the agricultural industry and produced a multitude of crops and commodities using sophisticated techniques and equipment. They grew 90 percent of marketed maize, the main staple; 90 percent of cotton, the main industrial crop; and virtually all tobacco and other export crops, including wheat, coffee, tea, and sugar, accounting in all for one-third of total exports. White farmers employed about one-third of the wage-earning labour force, some 271,000 people in 1980.

Numbering about 6,000, they were well organised, resourceful, and long accustomed to exerting influence to get their way. They had for years been the backbone of Ian Smith's Rhodesian Front, voting for him in one election after another, determined to protect their land interests. Mugabe saw the need to treat them as "royal game," awarding the industry generous price rises and other financial incentives, ensuring that technical services and support remained at a high standard, and proceeding with plans for land reform in a cautious and orderly manner.

But as his popularity faded and discontent over the government's manifest corruption and inefficiency spread, Mugabe turned on white farmers as the scapegoat for the country's ills, fanning grievances over land that had fuelled two previous wars.

When the Pioneer Column of white settlers arrived in Mashonaland in 1890, their main hope was to find gold. Each settler was awarded fifteen mining claims. The number of mining claims rose from 7,000 in 1891 to 160,000 in 1898. But the gold rush soon proved disappointing. The small white community therefore turned to the next available prize: land.

The scramble for land in the 1890s became little more than plunder. Farms were pegged out regardless of whether local people were living there. Initially Cecil Rhodes promised each of the 200 pioneers free farms of 1,500 morgen (3,175 acres). But a host of fortune-hunters—quasi-aristocrats, military men, and speculators—followed in their wake, grabbing land at every opportunity. The company's administrator, Leander Starr Jameson, encouraged them to take what land they wanted. Major Sir John Willoughby, who had been seconded from the Royal Horse Guards to act as chief staff officer to the Pioneer Column, was granted 600,000 acres in Mashonaland and bought up a large number of other land rights from pioneers who went off in search of gold. His company, Willoughby's Consolidated Company, eventually accumulated 1.3 million acres. Rhodes's surveyor-general, on taking up his post, was "awarded" 640,000 acres.

Missionaries were active too, acquiring almost a third of a million acres, with Catholics taking half of that. A young assistant working for the Anglican bishop of Mashonaland was soon exhausted by the constant search for more farms. "The one thing I strongly object to," he wrote to his parents in 1892, "is to go looking for more *farms*, which I hear ... is the Bishop's great idea. He already has more than 40!! All over 3,000 acres! And not one of them is being worked, either as farm or station as far as I can discover."

The bulk of the land was taken up by speculative companies. By 1899, some 9.3 million acres were in the hands of these companies. A new administrator, William Milton, who arrived in 1896, was appalled by the scale of land distribution. "Jameson has given nearly the whole country away to Willoughby's Whites and others of that class so that there is absolutely no land left which is of any value for settlement of Immigrants by Government." He stressed the need to "clear out the Honourable and military elements which are rampant everywhere." Within ten years of the arrival of the Pioneer Column, nearly 16 million acres—one-sixth of the entire land area of 96 million acres—had been seized by whites.

The land they took was mainly in the high veld of Mashonaland and Matabeleland and included much of the most fertile land in the country. But the difficulties they faced were immense. They suffered drought; locusts; rinderpest; east coast fever; malaria; and a shortage of labour, transport, and equipment. Many farms were left vacant; others were run as little more than market gardens for Salisbury, Bulawayo, and small mining centres.

The uprisings of 1896 brought the entire enterprise to a halt. First the Ndebele, then the Shona rose against white rule in one of the most violent, sustained, and highly organised episodes of resistance of the colonial era in Africa. The white casualty figures—372 killed and 129 wounded—represented about 10 percent of the white population. In Matabeleland, Rhodes eventually negotiated a peace settlement with the Ndebele. In Mashonaland, however, Shona chiefs were hunted down until the last pocket of resistance had been eliminated; there, no peace treaty was signed. As the British government later acknowledged, Rhodesia was established by right of conquest. Memories of the 1896–1897 revolt—or Chimurenga, as it was called by the Shona—lingered long enough for African nationalists to draw inspiration from it sixty years later.

In the wake of the revolt, white officials recognised that there was an urgent need to assign land for African use before any more land was taken by white settlers. Native reserves were set aside for "traditional" communal occupation. The intention was to use them as a temporary measure, but they soon became an established part of the pattern of land ownership. In Mashonaland, the reserves in 1910 totalled about 17 million acres, amounting to 37 percent of the total area of the province; about two-thirds of the Shona population found themselves living there. In Matabeleland, no more than 7.7 million acres were set aside, a mere 16 percent of the total area of the province, and of this 5.3 million acres comprised three waterless and largely uninhabited areas. In the Bulawayo district, once the heart of the Ndebele homeland, no reserve could be assigned because all the land had been taken by white settlers. Only one-third of the Ndebele population lived within the area established for reserves. In theory, Africans had the right to purchase land outside the reserves, but few possessed the means to do so. Initially, the black population, numbering about 750,000, was small enough to cope with this upheaval in land ownership. But as the population grew, the reserves became overcrowded.

The division of land between white and black was formalised in 1931 with the introduction of the Land Apportionment Act. White areas of Rhodesia were extended from 31 million to 48 million acres, although at the time some 7 million acres of white land, most of it within thirty-five miles of the line of rail, lay unoccupied and wholly undeveloped. Indeed, for the next forty years, white farmers never used more than 36 million acres of land assigned to them. The white farming areas included most of the best highveld land in the country, spreading north and south of the main road and railway between Bulawayo and Salisbury and between Salisbury and Umtali in the east, as well as swathes of ranching land in the semi-arid south and west.

The Land Apportionment Act stipulated that no African was entitled to hold or occupy land in white areas. Thus, half of the land area became the preserve of white farmers. Numbering no more than 2,500 in 1931, this elite group was given every encouragement and incentive by the government to develop and prosper.

The land area assigned for native reserves was reduced from 25 million acres in 1910 to 21.6 million acres, even though there were already signs of land degradation setting in. In addition, some 7.5 million acres were set aside as Native Purchase Areas for the use of master-farmers. The intention was to create a group of prosperous middle-class farmers who would act as a bulwark against radical elements. But some 4 million acres of Native Purchase Area land comprised five large, remote, low-lying areas, in some cases infested with tsetse flies; more than half of the area lay along the borders of the country, far from market towns.

The consequence of the Land Apportionment Act, which remained in force for nearly forty years, was that the black population, which numbered 1 million in 1931, was allocated 29 million acres, whereas the white population, numbering 48,000, of whom only 11,000 were settled on the land, were awarded 48 million acres. An area of 18 million acres of state land, which included forests and national parks, was left unassigned.

In the boom years that followed the end of the Second World War, white farmers benefited increasingly from technological advances made with improved machinery; new crop strains; and the use of fertilisers, herbicides, and pesticides. By switching to Virginia tobacco production, they found a reliable and highly profitable cash crop that had eluded them for forty years. An influx of immigrants raised the number of white farmers from 4,700 in 1945 to 8,600 in 1960. With more land needed for production, thousands of Africans were evicted from white farm areas and were forced into reserves that were already overcrowded. During the 1950s the African population rose from 2 to 3 million.

African grievances over land eventually swelled into nationalist protest. Facing rural unrest, the government of the day suggested that it might be necessary to remove the Land Apportionment Act to help defuse the nationalist tide. But white farmers would have none of it. In the 1962 election, when Ian Smith's Rhodesian Front promised to keep the Land Apportionment Act intact, they voted for the Front en masse, helping to propel it to victory.

In 1969 Smith introduced the Land Tenure Act, intending to entrench the division of land "for all time." In what purported to be an equitable solution, the white area henceforth comprised 45 million acres; the African area also comprised 45 million acres; the remaining 6 million acres included national parks and game reserves.

Thousands of Africans continued to be evicted from white farming areas. Most evictions passed unnoticed. But one defiant stand taken by a chief in the eastern highlands caught international attention.

The Tangwena people had lived in the Inyanga area for hundreds of years. In 1905, unknown to them, their ten square miles of land was sold by Rhodes's British South African Company to a private land company. In 1963 the Gaeresi Ranch Company, acting under pressure from the Rhodesian Front government, tried to evict the Tangwena. The Tangwena took their case to court, and the courts found in 1968 that they could not lawfully be moved. The government then issued a proclamation that effectively changed the law and ordered the Tangwena to move to another area known as Bende.

The Tangwena steadfastly refused to move. In 1969 the security forces burned down their homes, destroyed their crops, impounded their cattle, arrested men and women, and closed down their school.

As he watched his cattle being driven away, Chief Rekayi Tangwena was interviewed by a white reporter from a radical publication, *Struggle*.

"We are angry with what is happening," he said. "This land is ours and now they say that it does not belong to Africans. They arrested my people. They beat a pregnant woman—she is still in hospital to this day. The government will have to build a jail large enough to take all my people. We do not want to go to Bende. We want our cattle back on this land.

"It is the Europeans who have come to disturb us, to destroy our property, to deprive us of the wealth of this land. This is unforgivable. My people are heartsick. These cattle that they are driving away...they are trying to provoke my people, so that they may shoot us with their guns, because we are defenceless."

He was asked whether he saw himself as a politician, playing a more prominent political role.

I am not a politician. I simply want my rights. I think that this country should be freed so that every individual would have a say in government. If the Europeans were less cruel and oppressive in their government, we could determine our lives in consultation with one another. This would be good. The Europeans should not ill-treat us; kick us; say, this belongs to me, that belongs to me, everything belongs to me. Where was the African living when the Europeans first came? They found us here. Should we live in trees today? Every place that they find to be good they say belongs to them. Good and fertile land they want for themselves. As Africans we have been driven into the mountains. What is there for us to eat? Is this not destructive? It is.

We fear. We fear because they threaten to shoot us with guns. Where can we go? They arrest us and toast us on fires; they hit us with the butts of their guns. How can you say anything? If you open your mouth you are hit with the butt of a gun. They show you the gun and threaten to shoot. Where can we go? You have no option but to fear the gun that you can see....

The people must tell the government to stop their cruelty. We want a better system; we want a situation of love.

Chief Tangwena was charged under the Law and Order (Maintenance) Act for making a subversive statement. The reporter, Dr. Anthony McAdam, a former university lecturer, also faced prosecution and fled the country. The offices of a church newspaper, *Umbowo*, which published a poem about the eviction of the Tangwena people, were raided and its editor charged under the Law and Order (Maintenance) Act for "engendering feelings of hostility."

Rather than move to the new location at Bende, Tangwena and some 600 followers took to the hills. The Catholic Justice and Peace Commission adopted their cause, sending Sister Mary Aquina to the eastern highlands to investigate their plight. Sister Mary went first to stay at Nyafaru farm, an agricultural cooperative adjacent to the Tangwena land, then spent four days with the Tangwena people in the forest. "It was the first time in my life that I experienced the protection of Africans against fellow Europeans," she recalled.

In 1975, when Mugabe and Tekere needed an escape route from Salisbury, it was Sister Mary who helped them, lending them her car to reach Nyafaru farm to link up with Chief Tangwena. Tangwena himself guided them across the border into Mozambique and made contact with Frelimo officials, telling them Mugabe and Tekere had come on business: "war business."

The guerrilla war of the 1970s—the second Chimurenga, as the Shona called it—was fought principally to overthrow white rule and gain power, but land grievances and landlessness, the idea of winning back "lost" lands, provided much of the rhetoric and motivation behind it. In its initial phase, the guerrillas achieved widespread support in areas in the northeast—Centenary, Sipolilo, and Mount Darwin—where land had been taken over by whites only recently, in the postwar era, and where resentment over dispossession was still raw. Throughout the war, Mugabe promised that when whites were defeated, every African would be given land.

During the Lancaster House negotiations, the land issue was one of the most difficult to resolve. The whites, backed by the

British government, insisted that land rights were entrenched in a Bill of Rights in the new constitution. Mugabe was furious that Muzorewa would not support him in speaking out for African land claims. As he subsequently recalled,

I said, "But you are Africans, how dare you accept the position on land shall be governed by the Bill of Rights? We can't get anywhere with the Bill of Rights. Don't you remember your history? The land was never bought from us. Support our position on this one!" They said no, they could not. So at one time I said to Lord Carrington, "Look at them! What are they? Baa baa black sheep, have you any wool!" It took him time to unravel that but finally he got it.... They were black sheep, just saying "Baa Baa" to the master!

The compromise that Mugabe was forced to accept meant that for ten years the government could only purchase land against the owner's wishes if it was "underutilised" or required for a public purpose, and only then if the owner was provided with prompt and full compensation in foreign exchange. In other words, land transactions could only be conducted on a "willing seller–willing buyer" basis. This provision effectively restricted the government to purchasing limited and often poor-quality land that was voluntarily offered for sale. Britain agreed to help finance a land redistribution programme, but within a strict budget.

Mugabe took a pragmatic view of the arrangement:

We had...to compromise on certain fundamental principles, but only because there was a chance, in the future, to amend the position. We had got the main concession of the creation of democracy. There would be democratic elections in the country, and if a government was going to be yielded up by those elections, based on majority rule, then that government would, in due course, bring about the necessary changes. So we didn't worry very much. But it hurt us. We did not like it.

Thus, at independence in 1980, the pattern of land ownership remained much as it had been for most of the twentieth century: white large-scale commercial farmers, numbering some 6,000, held 39 percent of the land; black small-scale commercial farmers, numbering 8,000, held 4 percent; the communal lands where 4 million people lived accounted for 41 percent; and national parks and state forests accounted for 16 percent. Most of the productive land was possessed by whites; three-quarters of all peasant land lay in areas where droughts occurred frequently and where even normal levels of rainfall were inadequate for intensive crop production. In communal areas, the population density was more than three times that of "white" areas, and the number of people living there exceeded their carrying capacity by about 2 million people. Land shortage and land degradation were deeply entrenched problems. A university report warned: "Land degradation is widespread in many of these tribal areas and in some cases has reached such advanced stages that regeneration processes will take several decades to restore the vegetation and soil cover."

Upon taking office, Mugabe's government initiated a programme to resettle 18,000 families over a three-year period on some 2.5 million acres of former white land at a cost of £30 million (US $60 million), half of which was to be funded by the British government. The programme was elaborately designed and required an infrastructure of roads, fencing, dip tanks, housing, schools, and clinics. Most of the land acquired for resettlement comprised whole farms in the northeast that had been abandoned during the war. Hoping to achieve a faster rate of progress, the government announced in 1982 its intention to resettle at least 162,000 peasant families—more than 1 million people—over the next three years. It was a wildly ambitious target, far beyond the government's ability to implement. Even the original pace of resettlement faltered.

By the end of the first decade of independence, a total of 52,000 families, some 416,000 people, had been resettled on the 6.5 million acres of former white land the government had bought for the purpose. This was a worthy enough achievement, but it came nowhere near tackling the scale of the problem: Each year the communal areas alone produced an additional 40,000 families, compounding the problem of overcrowding.

Moreover, as government officials acknowledged, many resettlement schemes were failures. Resettled land was heavily under-utilised. Political interference plagued all levels of administration. Candidates were selected not on the basis of their farming ability but for other reasons. The entire programme suffered from a lack of technical support and was bogged down in massive bureaucracy. One document produced by the Department of Rural Development listed twenty-five ministries, departments, and parastatal organisations as having a role in the programme.

Mugabe occasionally resorted to rhetoric in addressing the problem. "We can never have peace in the country unless the peasant population is satisfied in relation to the [land] issue," he declared in 1981. But land resettlement was never one of Mugabe's priorities. Having raised expectations with grand announcements, the government sought to "de-emphasise" the issue, once the difficulties of achieving a faster rate of progress were clear. Zanu-PF politicians were anyway preoccupied with acquiring farms of their own. By 1990 a new class of landowners was firmly established: ministers, MPs, senior civil servants, police and defence officials, and parastatal managers. In all, they had managed to acquire 8 percent of commercial farmland since independence, although little of it was put to productive use.

With few demonstrable benefits to show after ten years of independence, Mugabe decided to whip up support over the land issue in advance of the 1990 election. "It makes absolute nonsense of our history as an African country that most of our arable and ranching land is still in the hands of our erstwhile colonisers, while the majority of our peasant community still live like squatters in their God-given land." He promised a "revolutionary" programme of agrarian reform to redistribute land.

Mugabe's programme of land reform in the 1990s was implemented in a chaotic manner from the start. No attempt was made to consult farmers, rural communities, or even the government's own agricultural specialists. In December 1990, amid singing and dancing, parliament passed a constitutional amendment that empowered the government simply to confiscate land, fix the price it paid, and deny the right to appeal to courts for fair compensation. The aim, said the government, was to acquire some 13 million acres of land—nearly half of the remaining white-owned land—on which to settle 110,000 families. "The white colonialists took our land without paying for it. Why should we pay them exorbitant prices?" Sabina Mugabe, the president's sister, told parliament. "Must we stay squatters on the land of our birth?" she asked. "Give them [whites] bikes and take back our land." The debate took on an ugly, racist tone.

Outside parliament, the legislation triggered a crisis for white farmers and brought a barrage of criticism against the government for trying to remove the right of legal appeal for a fair price. Zimbabwe's first black chief justice, Enoch Dumbutshena, who had recently retired, declared, "It flies in the face of all accepted norms of modern society, and the rule of law." Human rights groups such as the Catholic Commission for Justice and Peace protested, and Britain and the United States made clear their opposition. The legislation seemed likely not only to disrupt the entire agricultural industry but to deter foreign investors and the donor community.

Angry and anxious, some 4,000 white farmers from across the country descended on Harare in January 1991 for a meeting with the minister of agriculture, Witness Mangwende, organised by the Commercial Farmers Union (CFU). It was the largest gathering of whites since independence. CFU leaders stressed the importance of commercial agriculture, pointing out that it accounted for one-quarter of all jobs and 40 percent of export earnings. It was the engine that drove the economy. To force half the commercial farmers off their land without adequate compensation would cause incalculable damage both to the economy and to Zimbabwe's reputation abroad. They said they recognised the need for land redistribution but suggested that resettlement land should first come either from the half million acres of land the government already owned but had not distributed or from unproductive land, including farms owned by the black elite. They proposed joint boards to determine what land should be purchased for resettlement and an arbitration court to decide how much farmers should be paid.

Mangwende was unimpressed by such arguments. "The land question is a time bomb which must be solved now," he told the farmers. "The time for energy-consuming debates on the desirability or otherwise of this programme has run out. The only useful debate that the government is willing to entertain about the resettlement programme is on the implementation modalities." The matter was non-negotiable: "You will have to trust us."

In the following months the arguments over land became increasingly bitter, raising racial tensions in Zimbabwe and drawing in Britain, the United States, the World Bank, and the International Monetary Fund to defend the rights of white farmers. All warned that unless the government modified its position so as to assure property owners fair compensation, Zimbabwe would forfeit crucial aid packages.

Mugabe remained obdurate. He portrayed the issue as an historic reckoning between the land-hungry majority and "a greedy bunch of racist usurpers" determined to thwart the popular will. And he declared that he would disregard any court decision that might stand in the way of his land acquisition programme. "I, Robert Mugabe, cannot be dragged to court by a settler."

At the last minute, however, when presenting the Land Acquisition Bill to parliament in 1992, the government introduced an amendment that deleted from the bill a paragraph barring the courts from overturning a government assessment of the value of a confiscated farm "on the grounds that the compensation is not fair." Mangwende told parliament that productive farmers had nothing to fear from the legislation and that the main targets were under-utilised land, absentee landlords, foreign-owned derelict land, land owned merely for speculative purposes, and "people with more farms than are considered necessary."

On the basis of such reassurances, the CFU agreed to work with the government. "While many of these methods are not actually in-corporated into the Bill, if they are implemented along the lines de-scribed by the minister, the CFU will not be found wanting in co-operating with the government," said the CFU president, Alan Burl. In subsequent discussions, there appeared to be a consensus that the resettlement programme would focus first on derelict and underutilised farms.

Without warning or consultation, in July 1992 the government "designated" for acquisition thirteen farms totalling 17,000 acres in the Mutare district. Farmers learned of the decision from newspa-pers. Despite assurances that derelict or underutilised farms were the government's main targets, these farms were mostly productive. One was a major supplier of milk to Mutare; another was a leading tobacco producer; two belonged to black members of the Commer-cial Farmers Union. As an indication of how much planning had gone into the decision, seven of the thirteen farms were subse-quently "undesignated."

In 1993 the government designated another seventy farms cov-ering 475,000 acres for acquisition. Again, many were highly pro-ductive. The list also included a number of farms belonging to the government's political opponents, arousing suspicions that the land acquisition programme was being used to settle old political scores. The most notable example was Churu Farm on the outskirts of

Harare, owned by Ndabaningi Sithole, the original leader of Zanu and a longtime political adversary of Mugabe. Sithole had bought the 830-acre farm in 1979 and had subdivided it into 2,000 stands for accommodation, mostly for people from his own tribe, the Ndau. The government first claimed that Sithole did not own the property, then that the settlement of squatters on the farm represented a health hazard, risking pollution of nearby Lake Chivero, Harare's main water reservoir. Using the Land Acquisition Act, the government ordered the residents, some 4,000 families, to leave. The Catholic Commission for Justice and Peace intervened and obtained a High Court injunction, arguing that the Land Acquisition Act was being used as a punitive measure and a political weapon. But the government ignored the High Court injunction and ordered the police to "forcefully remove" the families if they failed to leave voluntarily. "The government is now dealing with thousands of homeless people from the street," said a government minister, Joseph Msika. "So let the Churu Farm settlers join their homeless colleagues on the streets and we will deal with them there." Some 20,000 people were subsequently evicted by riot police.

Another opposition politician who became a victim of the Land Acquisition Act was James Chikerema, who owned an 800-acre farm near Zvimba, Mugabe's home area. "It's a punishment because I stood against him and have never been a member of his party," said Chikerema.

Of the seventy farms the government designated, twenty-seven were subsequently undesignated. Farmers still facing expropriation lodged objections with the minister of agriculture, as they were entitled to do under the terms of the Act. A small group, however, decided to challenge the legality of the entire Act. They argued that the process of "designation" under the Act was unconstitutional and deprived owners of their rights to property. "Once designation has taken place, the farmer cannot sell, lease or dispose of his property, except with the permission of the minister. There is no right to approach the court. There is no right to appeal to an independent body except the minister. The minister becomes the court and appeal court."

Mugabe was furious at the challenge. "We will not brook any decision by any court from acquiring any land," he said in July 1993. "We will get land we want from anyone, be they black or white, and we will not be restricted to under-utilised land." Addressing Zanu-PF's central committee in September 1993, he threatened to seize land without paying any compensation. "If white settlers just took the land from us without paying for it, we can in a similar way just take it from them, without paying for it, or entertaining any ideas of legality and constitutionality. Perhaps our weakness has been the fact that we have tried to act morally and legally, when they acted immorally and illegally." He bitterly denounced Western governments that criticised his land policies. "How can these countries who have stolen land from the Red Indians, the Aborigines and the Eskimos dare to tell us what to do with our land?"

However, to Mugabe's acute embarrassment, the land resettlement programme was soon engulfed in scandal. In April 1994 an independent newspaper discovered that one of the farms the government had forcibly purchased against the white owner's objections—a 3,000-acre farm in Hwedza—had been used not for the resettlement of thirty-three landless peasants as intended but leased out to Witness Mangwende, the former agriculture minister who had so aggressively pushed through the Land Acquisition Act and who currently served as minister of education. Nothing illustrated so graphically the greed that motivated the ruling clique.

In an attempt to ward off a public outcry, the current minister of agriculture, Kumbirai Kangai, told parliament that the Hwedza farm had been leased to Mangwende under a "tenant resettlement" scheme designed to promote indigenous commercial farming through leasing state farms to individuals. The purpose, he said, was to "facilitate a more balanced racial composition of the large-scale farming sector." But no information about this scheme had previously been disclosed. It had been operated in secret. Under questioning, Kangai refused to divulge any names.

Further newspaper investigations revealed that scores of government-owned farms intended for resettlement had been handed out on leases to ministers and senior officials. Among the beneficiaries were Charles Utete, the powerful head of Mugabe's office; Perence Shiri, the air force commander who had once commanded 5 Brigade; Augustine Chihuri, the commissioner of police; and Solomon Tawengwa, Harare's first executive mayor. In many cases, only nominal rents had been charged; in some cases, no rent at all.

Bowing to popular outrage, Mugabe agreed to cancel seventy-two farm leases. "The land should not have been leased out in the first place," he said. Yet once the furore had died down, the black elite continued to get their hands on government land, leaving the redistribution exercise contaminated by corruption. Britain, having spent £44 million on land resettlement since independence, decided to cut off further support for it.

The land scandal added to the government's growing unpopularity. While the population at large faced rising unemployment, high inflation, and deteriorating social services, Mugabe and the ruling elite were seen to be using every opportunity to enrich themselves. Following the 1995 election, Mugabe increased the size of his cabinet from twenty-nine to forty-two ministers, in defiance of the World Bank, the IMF, and Western donors, who had urged him to slim down the cabinet and drastically curb government spending. The World Bank suggested that no more than fifteen ministers were needed for the cabinet to function effectively. To compound the extravagance, the cabinet then awarded Mugabe, all ministers, and members of parliament lavish pay increases of 133 percent, while at the same time cutting health spending by 43 percent and limiting civil servants to 20 percent pay increases and eliminating their annual bonuses.

A glimpse of the public anger lying beneath the surface came in November 1995 when street riots and looting suddenly broke out in Harare, a city previously renowned for its orderly and peaceful character. The trouble started when police chasing two suspected thieves opened fire with an assault rifle, killing two passersby and injuring a third. An infuriated crowd overturned a police van and set it alight, then went on to destroy eight more government vehicles.

The potential for street violence was considerable. Each year some 200,000 youths left school searching for work. Yet since 1990 the increase in the number of formal sector jobs annually had been no more than 15,000. At least one-third of the labour force was unemployed. In protests against declining living standards, civil servants, doctors, and nurses staged strikes; students boycotted classes.

Mugabe's reaction to the country's economic woes was predictably to blame the whites. "It is sad to note that a majority of our industrialists are crooks," he declared during his 1996 presidential election campaign. "Some are using retrenchment as a cost reduction measure thereby increasing their profit margins at the expense of Zimbabweans." He accused them of evading taxes and fraudulently transferring money out of the country.

The white community in general became the target of increasing abuse. Although numbering no more than 80,000, they still controlled most of the mines and manufacturing industry as well as commercial agriculture. Many were Zimbabwean citizens and had long since shed the old racial attitudes of white Rhodesians. But their social contact with blacks tended to be minimal. They represented a rich elite that were far more readily identifiable than Mugabe's own.

Whereas Mugabe had once focused attention on the government's record in health, education, and social services, now he used anti-white antagonism as the centrepiece of his strategy. He called

for the "indigenisation of the economy," adding that some Zimbabweans were "more indigenous than others." Addressing party members, he said: "Our people still suffer economic disablement as a
result of myriad old laws, business practice and prejudices, themselves a legacy of the colonial past that sought a wholesale disem-
powerment of the blacks. Needless to say this situation is
unacceptable and cannot be allowed to continue."

Government-controlled newspapers, notably the *Sunday Mail*,
unleashed a torrent of racist attacks against whites, claiming that all
whites were racist and denouncing them for trying to "perpetuate
economic domination." Large advertisements appeared in the press
written by Zanu-linked organisations and by businessmen like
Roger Boka lambasting whites for being "filthy rich" and "arrogant."

Foreign critics were given short shrift. If foreign investors ob-
jected to anti-white statements, said Mugabe, then they could "take
their money and fly away." As for criticism of government over-
spending and extravagance, he retorted that he would do as he saw
fit "and not dance to the whims and caprices of the World Bank and
IMF."

Another group whom Mugabe singled out for abuse was the homosexual community. Mugabe's growing preoccupation with homosexuals stemmed partly from his own innate conservatism. But
he also believed that militant homophobia would be a popular
move, distracting attention from more pressing domestic issues. In
traditional Shona culture, much importance was attached to marriage and child-bearing. Anyone who side-stepped these rites of
passage was likely to be marked down as a misfit or social outcast.
No open discussions of homosexuality occurred. Mugabe portrayed
homosexuality as "un-African," an import from Europe to be despised and rejected.

The event that triggered public controversy over the issue was
an international book fair in Harare in August 1995. It was the

largest publishing conference ever held in Africa, with 240 exhibi-
tions representing 450 publishers from thirty-eight countries. Two
Nobel laureates from Africa, Nadine Gordimer and Wole Soyinka,
had been invited to participate. The fair's theme was "Human
Rights and Justice," with seminars planned on the freedom of expression and freedom of the press.

Mugabe was scheduled to open the fair until he learned that one
of the exhibitors was a group called Gays and Lesbians of Zimbabwe (Galz). Mugabe insisted that Galz should be evicted. "Zimbabwean society and government do not accept the public display of
homosexual literature and material," said a government spokesman.
"The trustees of the book fair should not, therefore, force the val-
ues of gays and lesbians on to the Zimbabwean culture."

Once Galz had been duly evicted, Mugabe proceeded to open
the fair with a blistering assault on homosexuals. He described
them as sodomists and sexual perverts who had no rights. Zimbabwe, he said, had a "formidable" set of morals and taboos that it
could not abandon unless its society decided they were no longer
needed:

> I find it extremely outrageous and repugnant to my human con-
> science that such immoral and repulsive organisations, like those of
> homosexuals who offend both against the law of nature and the
> morals and religious beliefs espoused by our society, should have
> any advocates in our midst and even elsewhere in the world.... If
> we accept homosexuality as a right, as is being argued by the associ-
> ation of sodomists and sexual perverts, what moral fibre shall our
> society ever have to deny organised drug addicts, or even those
> given to bestiality, the rights they might claim and allege they pos-
> sess under the rubrics of "individual freedom" and "human rights,"
> including the freedom of the press, to write, publish and publicise
> their literature?

He concluded: "We don't believe they have any rights at all."

When human rights groups protested against such bigotry, Mugabe responded vitriolically, describing homosexuals as "worse than dogs and pigs"; they were "beasts," he said, "guilty of sub-human behaviour"; he asked people to help the police "to root the evil out." A group of seventy U.S. congressmen who sent him a letter of condemnation were given short shrift. "Let the Americans keep their sodomy, bestiality, stupid and foolish ways to themselves, out of Zimbabwe," Mugabe told a crowd of supporters. "We don't want those practices here. Let them be gay in the United States, Europe and elsewhere. They shall be sad people here."

By the mid-1990s Mugabe had become an irascible and petulant dictator, brooking no opposition, contemptuous of the law and human rights, surrounded by sycophantic ministers and indifferent to the incompetence and corruption around him. His record of economic management was lamentable. He had failed to satisfy popular expectations in education, health, land reform, and employment. And he had alienated the entire white community.

Yet all the while Mugabe continued to believe in his own greatness. Isolated and remote from ordinary reality, possessing no close friends and showing clear signs of paranoia, he listened only to an inner circle of conspiratorial aides and colleagues. Whatever difficulties occurred he attributed to old enemies—Britain, the West, the old Rhodesian network—all bent, he believed, on destroying his "revolution." He was convinced he could overcome any challenge they posed, just as he had done during the war.

What he was not prepared for, however, was a revolt that erupted from inside Zanu's citadel, from a group he had assumed were his most loyal supporters: the war veterans.

# [8]

# ENTER THE WAR VETERANS

WHAT PROPELLED the war veterans into action was yet another corruption scandal. Murmurs of discontent over Mugabe's neglect of war veteran issues had been growing steadily louder. In December 1996, at the funeral of a popular war veteran, Mukoma Musa, a serving army officer, Brigadier Gibson Mashingaidze, delivered a forthright attack on Zanu-PF, questioning its commitment to the ideals and principles it had set for itself during the war. While the politicians had enriched themselves, said the brigadier, veterans like Musa had been ignored. He told mourners that he had had to spend $10,000 of his own money to give Musa a decent burial because he was so poor. "Some people now have ten farms to their names and luxury yachts and have developed fat stomachs when ex-combatants like Comrade Musa lived in abject poverty. Is this the Zanu-PF I trusted with my life? Is this the same party which promised to care for us in our old age? ... To the majority of Zimbabweans I say our party, which I believe is still a great party, has abandoned us."

Three months later the government was forced to suspend disbursements from the War Victims Compensation Fund because the fund had been looted so thoroughly there was nothing left to make further payments. An amount of $450 million (US $40 million) set aside for the current financial year had gone in eight months. There were suspicions that in previous years the fund had been pilfered in the same way. A massive $1.5 billion had been paid out between 1992 and 1997, much of it in dubious circumstances. The culprits were said to include senior politicians, officials, and their relatives.

The issue was taken up in parliament by the independent MP Margaret Dongo. Overcoming attempts by Zanu-PF to thwart her, she tabled a motion calling on the auditor-general to investigate the missing funds. "The whole thing is scandalous because most of the people who received the money did not deserve to get anything," she said. To the dismay of Zanu-PF chefs, more than a hundred MPs decided to support Dongo's motion.

The War Veterans Association also began to agitate for their money. The campaign was led by Chenjerai Hunzvi, a devious and corrupt activist who was himself directly involved in the scam. His own war record was suspect. He claimed to have been a key member of Zapu's high command during the war, but senior Zapu officials denied it, saying he had been no more than an ordinary Zapu official who had never seen combat. After working in Zapu headquarters in Lusaka, he had left for Poland in 1978 to study medicine. While attending Warsaw University, he had met and married a Polish woman, with whom he had two children. In her account of the marriage in a book titled *White Slave*, published in 1994, the wife described him as an "unfaithful, vain sadist" who beat her regularly. She also pointed out that during the war he had "never held a gun."

Hunzvi claimed he had qualified as a doctor in Poland in 1990. After returning to Zimbabwe, he worked in a government hospital in Harare. In 1995 he was assigned to be an assessor to produce medical reports on ex-combatants claiming compensation for injuries sustained in the war. Under the terms of the War Victims Compensation Act, ex-combatants were entitled to claim a disability "percentage" for each of their injuries, whether it was the loss of

an eye, a finger, or even a toenail; the sum of the injuries constituted a claimant's total disability percentage. The role of assessor
gave Hunzvi a decisive say not only over gauging the extent of injuries of claimants and hence their income but also over who was el-
igible, opening up a potential gold mine for himself and others keen
to exploit the fund. Having gained this foothold in the war veteran
world, Hunzvi ascended rapidly to become chairman of the War
Veterans Association, using it as the route to political power and influence.

When the government dithered over addressing war veteran
grievances and Mugabe turned down requests to meet them, Hunzvi decided on direct action. War veterans were sent to harangue
ministers and party officials. Mugabe tried to appease them by appointing a commission of inquiry under Judge Godfrey Chidyausiku to investigate the missing funds and by promising to resume
their payments. But the war veterans were not satisfied. For three
successive days in July 1997, hundreds took to the streets of Harare,
some on crutches, some dressed in rags. On the first day they
forced three ministers to leave a public meeting under police protection. On the second day they marched on Mugabe's office,
chanting "Chimurenga! Chimurenga!" On the third day they descended on an international conference centre where Mugabe was
hosting a conference for African American investors, singing revolutionary songs, banging drums, waving placards, and denouncing
Mugabe himself.

Mugabe tried to put a bold face on the situation. He ascribed the
demonstrations "to economic difficulties that exist in this country
where economic benefits have remained in the hands of a minority
and not accrued to the majority." And he still refused to meet the
war veterans.

The next incident was even more humiliating. At the commem-
oration of Heroes' Day at the National Heroes' Acre on August 11,
Mugabe's speech was nearly drowned out by war veterans banging

drums and chanting. Instead of his usual hour-long address, Mugabe spoke for only ten minutes. When ministers accused the war veterans of showing "a lack of respect" for the president and described them as "rebels" and "bandits," they retaliated by ransacking party headquarters.

The independent press was sympathetic to their cause. The *Zimbabwe Independent* commented,

> Like the rest of the population, the liberation war heroes are victims of a corrupt political system that clearly does not have public concerns at heart. They long ago lost the drive to solve problems that the public experiences, particularly if there is no personal gain in such pursuits. The nation finds itself in a desperate power vacuum as those vested with power and authority fail to exercise it to benefit the electorate. Their main preoccupation is self-enrichment and everything else later.

By the time Mugabe agreed to a meeting on August 21, the war veterans had become increasingly aggressive. Their demands included not just a resumption of payments from the Compensation Fund but gratuities of $50,000 and monthly pensions of $2,000 for each of the 50,000 veterans claiming compensation. They also demanded land, threatening to occupy white-owned farms if the government failed to give it to them. "In order to resolve this issue peacefully, we demand that 50 per cent of all ex-combatants needing settlement be given land by December 1997, the rest by July 1998," they told Mugabe. "Failure to meet these deadlines will force war veterans to move in and settle themselves on farms that have been identified for resettlement. They will occupy white man's land because the white man did not buy that land." Mugabe promised that the cabinet would discuss the matter.

To his further embarrassment, the Chidyausiku commission of inquiry into the scam acquired evidence of how it had extended to his own family. After a medical assessment carried out by Hunzvi, Mugabe's brother-in-law, Reward Marufu, an official in the president's office, had been awarded $822,668 (about US $70,000) on the basis of "a scar on his left knee" and "ulcers," adding up to a 95 percent disability. As soon as the scandal had come to light, Marufu had been sent off on a diplomatic posting to Canada to avoid questioning. Hunzvi himself had been awarded a total of $517,536 (US $43,300) after making four claims for "impaired hearing" and "sciatic pains of the thigh." For the first three claims, amounting to an 85 percent disability, he had been paid $361,620; when the fourth claim amounting to $155,916 was included, Hunzvi's disability rating had been recorded as 117 percent. He claimed he had sustained a thigh injury when he was struck by shrapnel from mortar bombs in an attack by Rhodesian forces on Zapu headquarters in Lusaka in 1977.

The list of other recipients sounded like a roll-call of the elite—ministers and officials—claiming such disabilities as aching feet, loss of appetite, backache, and blisters; the two most common conditions were "mental stress disorder" and "poly arthritis." The commissioner of police, Augustine Chihuri, was awarded $138,645 for "toe dermatitis of the right and left foot"; the air force commander, Perence Shiri, who had commanded 5 Brigade in Matabeleland, was awarded $90,249 for "poly arthritis and mental stress disorder"; the commander of the defence forces, Vitalis Zvinavashe, was awarded $224,395 for "skin allergy and chest injuries"; minister Joyce Mujuru was awarded $389,472 for "poor vision" and "mental stress disorder." Many of the dockets on politicians were "missing."

In the face of such evidence of corruption by his own colleagues, Mugabe capitulated to the war veterans. In addition to the gratuities and pensions they demanded, he promised them a package of land for resettlement, free health care, and free education. This bought him time, but it presented the government with a severe financial headache. The estimated cost was at least $4 billion, money that the government, already overspent, did not have. Mugabe said the government would use any means to get the money, borrowing it, if necessary, and dismissed concerns about a financial collapse. "Have you ever heard of a country that collapsed because of borrowing?" he asked. The World Bank was sufficiently worried to suspend its lending programme. And when Mugabe announced in November that the war veterans would be paid by Christmas, the value of the Zimbabwe dollar plunged.

Although temporarily appeasing the war veterans, Mugabe's capitulation showed Hunzvi how useful mob rule could be. When he was called before the Chidyausiku commission on November 8 to explain his role in the scam, Hunzvi ensured that the courtroom at the High Court where Judge Chidyausiku was presiding was packed with his own supporters. After admitting that he had signed medical forms for one of his relatives, Hunzvi argued that he had done nothing wrong in assessing claimants for disability allowances even if they were friends or relatives. He accused the commission of employing colonialist tactics of oppression. "It seems you have already planned to incriminate me. . . . Is it a crime to be a war veteran? . . . Is it a crime to assist war veterans?" he asked amid applause from his supporters. He claimed the commission was singling him out for attention rather than tackling more prominent figures. His supporters raised placards stating WHY HUNZVI ONLY, WHAT ABOUT REWARD MARUFU and $50,000 TODAY OR ELSE WAR. Some started shouting abuse, forcing the judge to adjourn the session to clear the court. Hunzvi's supporters then broke into song and danced on tables and witness stands. The commission held no further public hearings.

The war veterans crisis also reignited the land issue. With demands for land ringing in his ears, Mugabe resumed his attacks on white farmers. "We are going to take the land and we are not going to pay a cent to any soul," he said in October. "The colonial exercise of robbery will be corrected once and for all." He vowed that the government would take 12 million acres from white farmers for re-distribution to blacks. The only payment the government would make would be for buildings and for what he termed "infrastruc-tural development" like roads and dams, but nothing for "the soil it-self." It was up to Britain, as the former colonial power, to provide other compensation. "If Britain wants us to compensate its chil-dren, it must give us the money, or it does the compensation itself."

On November 28, 1997, the government published a list of 1,503 farms to be expropriated. The properties on the list totalled about 12 million acres and represented about 45 percent of the land held by Zimbabwe's 4,500 commercial farmers. By government fiat, the farmers lost their title to the land, their ability to borrow money using the land as collateral, and even their right to harvest crops. Those with "genuine grounds" were invited to lodge their objec-tions with the ministry. "We fought for the land and now we are going to take it," Mugabe told party supporters.

The shockwaves from this nationalisation of almost half the country's farmland reverberated throughout Zimbabwe and be-yond. Economists, bankers, and businessmen, white and black alike, warned that such a hasty, ill-planned move to seize so much of the country's productive assets would send it into an economic tailspin. The stock exchange, where more than a third of companies listed were heavily dependent on agriculture, plummeted. Britain rejected demands for further aid for the land resettlement programme, pointing out that the funds previously committed had failed to ben-efit poor blacks as had been intended. "We are willing to help, but only on the basis that land distribution should first of all be geared towards the poor people—that is, towards poverty alleviation," said a British minister.

When Mugabe tried to impose new taxes and levies to pay for his largesse towards the war veterans, he provoked mass resistance. Leading the campaign against him was Morgan Tsvangirai, the trade union leader, who had become one of Mugabe's most relentless critics. Since taking office as secretary-general of the Zimbabwe Congress of Trade Unions (ZCTU) in 1988, he had turned the labour confederation into a cohesive movement of twenty-seven unions with a membership of 400,000, one-third of the formal labour force. His crusade against the waste, extravagance, and corruption of the ruling elite, when workers were suffering an inexorable decline in the value of their wages, had made him a popular figure. He castigated the government for being "top-down, centralised and not accountable to people." He demanded that the elite cut back on their own lavish spending before taxing workers. "If state revenue is limited, so be the expenditure. Cut down on Mercs, Pajeros, ministers, embassies and perks. Stop corruption. Live within your means."

His own lifestyle was notably modest. He lived with his wife and six children in a comfortable house with worn furniture in a middle-class neighbourhood and drove a Mazda; his clothes were often rumpled. Born in 1952, he had grown up in a poor rural family in Buhera in Manicaland, left school early to work in a textile mill in Mutare, then moved to a nickel mine in Bindura in 1974, where he had become active in the mining union. His arrest and detention during the student protests of 1989 had brought him national prominence. When questioned about his lack of a university education, Tsvangirai retorted, "The government has lots of people with degrees and doctorates, but they are not doing such a good job of running the country."

Responding to the public fury at Mugabe's proposed tax increases, Tsvangirai organised a day of protest on December 9. Workers supported his call for a "stay-away" in the thousands, bringing many towns to a halt. Despite a High Court order permitting people to demonstrate peacefully, riot police broke up groups of protesters with tear-gas and baton charges. The government accused the white community of fomenting anti-government dissent in an attempt to thwart its programme of land acquisition. Two days after the protest, as Tsvangirai was working late in his office on the tenth floor of a shabby building in downtown Harare, seven Mugabe supporters walked in and beat him unconscious, fleeing only at the unexpected arrival of a secretary.

In January 1998, after a series of food price increases, riots broke out in Harare and several other towns. The price of maize meal, the main staple, had risen by 36 percent in October and 24 percent in December. In January the price of cooking oil and rice more than doubled; other commodities increased by 20 percent. The final straw was an announcement by the government's grain board of a further increase in the price of maize meal of 21 percent. The ensuing riots were the worst urban violence since independence. To quell them, Mugabe had to turn to the army for help, bringing troops on the streets for the first time. The impact on the business sector was severe. The stock exchange slumped. The Zimbabwe dollar, which had been worth 40 U.S. cents in 1990, sank to 5 cents. Yet there was no end to the government's profligacy.

In the same week as the food riots, the government spent more than US $2 million acquiring fifty new ministerial Mercedes-Benz cars. Ten days later it put forward legislation to provide sumptuous retirement benefits for Mugabe, his wife, and their children, as well as the country's two vice-presidents and their children. The Presidential Pension and Retirement Benefits Amendment Bill proposed to give Mugabe and his family substantial increases in pensions, plus free vehicles, air travel, bodyguards, medical attention, and staff for the rest of their lives.

In another trial of strength, the ZCTU organised a nationwide "stay-away" in March, ignoring a government warning that it was illegal. Blaming the white community for instigating the strike, Hunzvi threatened to march to the wealthy suburbs of Harare to confront them. He described the ZCTU as the "stooges and puppets" of white business.

Mugabe tried to dismiss Tsvangirai as a nonentity, in terms that revealed how arrogant and overmighty he had become. "You have the misplaced belief that you are more powerful than the government," he said. "People must weigh themselves and see what they are good at. Some drive trains, some are foremen.... People who witnessed the liberation struggle will not accept you [as leaders]."

Even within the Zanu hierarchy, however, there were growing misgivings about Mugabe's leadership. Party delegates at the annual conference roundly condemned the government's attempts to raise taxes. "*Hatidi!*—We don't want it!" they chorused when Mugabe put the proposal to them. In an unprecedented move in parliament on February 10, Dzikamayi Mavhaire, the MP for Masvingo Central and party chairman of Masvingo province, moved a motion to amend the constitution, arguing that the president's term of office should be limited to two five-year terms, instead of an unlimited number of six-year terms. "The president must go," he told parliament. The government newspaper, the *Herald*, ran an editorial urging the government to stop blaming white farmers and industrialists for the country's ills and work for more positive solutions. Mugabe retaliated by removing the editor and firing Mavhaire from party office. At a central committee meeting, he raged against "infidels, evil schemers and political saboteurs" within Zanu-PF who were conspiring to overthrow his government. Fearful of the consequences, no one else in the party spoke out.

For all Mugabe's bravado, Zimbabwe was sinking ever deeper into an economic crisis that he could not ignore. Desperate for loans from the World Bank, the IMF, and the European Union, he signed undertakings effectively shelving his plan to expropriate white-owned farms. In March 1998 the agriculture minister, Kumbirai Kangai, declared at a meeting of Western donors that no productive land would be seized, that white farmers would be compensated for the full value of any confiscated land, and that land reform would be carried out in accordance with the law and in a transparent manner.

The test of Mugabe's real intentions on the land issue came in September 1998 when a major international effort was made to find a workable solution.

Representatives from United Nations agencies; the International Monetary Fund; the World Bank; the European Union; and twenty-three foreign governments, including Britain, the United States, China, and Cuba, gathered for a three-day conference in Harare, along with local delegates from the Commercial Farmers Union, nongovernmental organisations (NGOs), civic groups, and other stakeholders, to draw up a new economic programme. All were agreed on the urgent need for land reform and resettlement.

Mugabe opened the conference by outlining ambitious plans for massive change. In the eighteen years since independence, the government had resettled some 70,000 families on about 9 million acres of land. What Mugabe proposed henceforth was to acquire a further 12 million acres on which to settle 150,000 families over a five-year period. The cost was estimated at Z $40 billion (then about US $2 billion). He urged the donor community to back the plan. "If we delay, the people will resettle themselves in any way they deem necessary," he warned. "It has happened before and it can happen again, so we hope that the Zimbabwe government's efforts to achieve orderly resettlement will receive your support."

The conference delegates considered Mugabe's proposals to be far too ambitious, well beyond the government's ability to implement. In view of the scandals that had been uncovered about the previous land programme, they also insisted that any new programme be strictly supervised to ensure that land was directed towards peasant settlement. Moreover, they stipulated that land had to be bought at market-related prices and on a willing seller–willing buyer basis. And instead of a massive programme of acquisition, they wanted a limited initial phase, carried out step-by-step, to ascertain its viability.

What was finally agreed to by all parties involved in the conference, including the Zimbabwe government, was a resettlement plan beginning with 118 farms, covering about 700,000 acres, already offered for sale by their white owners. The period of implementation was to be two years. Provided the programme was successful, it would be continued. The first step was to be the formation of a Technical Support Unit, financed by the UN Development Programme, which would act as a clearinghouse for the programme.

Two weeks later, keen to get the programme underway, a consultative committee of twelve donors willing to contribute funds met in Harare with government representatives to plan ahead. The donors included the World Bank, the UN Development Programme, the UN Food and Agriculture Organisation, the European Union, Britain, the United States, Australia, Denmark, Germany, Japan, Norway, and Sweden. It was the greatest opportunity that Mugabe had ever been given to make real progress on the land issue.

But nothing happened. The Technical Support Unit was never formed. In November, without warning, the agriculture minister, Kumbirai Kangai, abruptly announced the seizure of 841 white-owned farms.

Land for Mugabe was a political weapon. He had used it successfully during the war to help him gain power; he used it now to help keep him in power. With a population growing ever more disgruntled and restless after eighteen years of his rule, it was the last political card he had to play.


In June 1998, a year after its appointment, the Chidyausiku commission of inquiry into the defrauding of the War Victims Compensation Fund presented its findings to Mugabe. A long list of suspects was provided, including ministers and senior officials, whom Chidyausiku recommended should be prosecuted. But only one person was ever brought to book: Chenjerai Hunzvi. Hunzvi's fraud was too obvious to be ignored. Commenting at the time that Chidyausiku delivered his report, the Catholic Commission for Justice and Peace singled out Hunzvi's role as chairman of the War Veterans Association when urging the government to take stern measures against the looters. "It is shocking that a person in Hunzvi's position should intend to subvert the law regarding the fraudulent applications to the War Victims Fund."

Hunzvi was charged with forging medical reports, which had enabled him to claim $517,537 for suffering a 117 percent disability. But he was eventually acquitted. Explaining his verdict, Justice Paddington Garwe said, "The court has pointed to a number of unsatisfactory features in the evidence and conduct of Hunzvi. At most, therefore, all that one can say is that Hunzvi may well have been up to no good. But beyond that, one cannot say with certainty."

Nearly four years after the scandal first erupted, another High Court judge, George Smith, pointed out that the government had taken virtually no action to recover the $450 million looted from the fund, mainly by senior officials. "Why is it that those responsible for recovering the stolen money and punishing the offenders have done little, if anything, about it?" he asked. "They are ignoring their duties and should be held accountable." He continued: "Since millions of dollars of public money were stolen and many of the offenders and officials who ordered them are known, one wonders why nothing is being done."

Smith ordered the government to recover the stolen funds, drawing attention in particular to Reward Marufu, the president's brother-in-law, who had obtained $822,618, the highest claim from the fund, for "a scar on his left knee."

Nothing was done.

# [9]

## CONGO RICHES

EVEN WHILE Zimbabwe was descending in a spiral of decline, Mugabe still pursued his ambitions on the international stage. During the 1980s he had become accustomed to playing a central role in the alliance of Front Line States opposed to South Africa's apartheid regime. With the release of Nelson Mandela from prison in 1990 and his election as president in 1994, Mugabe's status was much diminished. He could no longer claim support and financial assistance from Western governments on the basis of his defiant stand against apartheid. Western attention was switched to ensuring that South Africa's fledgling democracy prospered. By comparison to Mugabe's increasingly wayward dictatorship, Nelson Mandela's accommodating style of leadership was considered infinitely preferable.

Mugabe was nevertheless determined to remain an international player. During the 1990s he travelled constantly, visiting 151 countries, invariably accompanied by a huge retinue of ministers, aides, and bodyguards, absent from Zimbabwe for weeks on end. He maintained a large foreign service abroad, staffed with loyal functionaries.

But the focus of his efforts was on southern Africa. In 1996 he succeeded in gaining control as chairman of the new defence arm of the Southern African Development Community (SADC), which had replaced the old Front Line States organisation. From this position he set out to assert himself as the region's principal power broker, seizing on the opportunity that the Congo's civil war presented.

Without consulting parliament or the cabinet, Mugabe decided in August 1998 to send troops to the Congo to prop up the tottering regime of Laurent Kabila, which was under attack by rebel forces advancing from the eastern Congo. As chairman of SADC's defence arm, Mugabe persuaded Namibia and Angola to join him, portraying their intervention as a SADC initiative. Initially, Zimbabwe deployed 3,000 troops, along with combat aircraft and armoured vehicles, but the number eventually increased to 11,000. When questioned about the cost to Zimbabwe, estimated to be at least US $1 million per day, Mugabe retorted, "Don't talk of resources as if resources are more important than the security of the people and the sovereignty of the country. The people must survive. The only way to bring peace to the country is to confront the rebels."

The folly of intervening in a distant foreign war in which Zimbabwe had no interest, at a time when the country's finances were in a ruinous state and the government was heavily over-borrowed, was evident to all. Both at home and abroad, the Congo intervention was seen as a sign of Mugabe's growing megalomania. Opinion polls showed it to be deeply unpopular. Western governments queried the need for providing Mugabe with financial assistance for land reform if he was prepared to squander money on foreign adventures.

For a select group of defence officials and businessmen, however, the Congo offered rich pickings. In return for military support, Kabila was prepared to hand out mining and timber concessions and offer preferential trade in diamonds, cobalt, and other minerals. The intention was said to be to allow Zimbabwe to recoup some of the cost of the war, but the beneficiaries tended to be members of the ruling elite. Numerous deals were struck over the supply of arms, ammunition, food, and consumer goods. At the centre of the Congo network was Emmerson Mnangagwa, Zanu-PF's business controller. Another key figure was John Bredenkamp, a former Rhodesian sanctions-buster and millionaire arms dealer. General Vitalis Zvina-vashe, the armed forces commander, who owned a transport busi-ness, won contracts to haul supplies to the Congo. To keep the army content, special allowances were paid to all soldiers serving in the Congo. Officers and other ranks were also encouraged to make their own deals, usually involving consumer goods. "There are fortunes to be made in the Congo," said Colonel Tshinga Dube on television. "They import everything there, even potatoes and cooking oil," he added, "so why rush to conquer the rebels?"

There were nevertheless military setbacks in the Congo. Rebel forces inflicted humiliating defeats on Kabila and his allies in Octo-ber 1998, killing and capturing Zimbabwean soldiers. Casualty fig-ures overall were kept secret, but rumours began to circulate in Harare of serious disarray within the military. Senior officers were said to have refused to obey orders. There was talk of mutinies and desertions.

On January 10, 1999, the independent Sunday newspaper, the *Standard*, reported that twenty-three officers and soldiers had been arrested in December for plotting a coup against Mugabe's govern-ment. The plotters, said the *Standard*, believed that their command-ing officers were more interested in pursuing business deals in the Congo than in the welfare of the soldiers fighting there.

The report would eventually have passed by but for the govern-ment's furious reaction. Quivering with rage, the defence minister, Moven Mahachi, denounced the *Standard* as part of an "unscrupu-lous media who are corrupt, liars and greedy to make money at all costs." He accused the reporters of "trying to bring down the gov-ernment, the economy and prevent investment." And he warned that they would not be allowed to get away with such "traitorous" stories.

The events that followed showed in clear detail how contemptuous of the law, the judiciary, and human rights Mugabe's government had become. The editor of the *Standard*, Mark Chavunduka, was held by military intelligence officers and CIO agents in an army barracks in Harare for ten days. His interrogators were initially restrained. "They said they had nothing against me, my newspaper and the staff but claimed the story had tarnished the image of the army and the country. I said if I was wrong then I would publish an apology and clarify the issue. They protested vigorously and said the story was not false but inaccurate in some respects. They said: 'We are interested in the sources of the story within the army.'" On the third day, they started beating him. On the fifth day he was taken to a basement with blood on the walls. "Do you think your blood is more special than that which is on the walls?" he was asked. He was beaten with a plank and given electric shock treatment on his genitals. On the eighth day he was finally taken to a police station, where he was allowed contact for the first time with a lawyer, his parents, and the *Standard*'s managing director, Clive Wilson. But then the police allowed him to be handed back to the army.

Chavunduka was taken back to the army barracks, along with the reporter who had written the offending article, Ray Choto. Later that night they were stripped naked, then kicked, punched, and beaten with planks. They were then driven to another location where they were electrocuted while in leg irons, their heads were wrapped in plastic bags and submerged in a water tank in mock drownings, and they were severely beaten. "Ray was taken into a different room and tortured so badly he screamed so much. They tortured us in a marathon session and at one time I thought he had died. He cried out a lot and suddenly went quiet."

Attempts to get access to Chavunduka were thwarted again and again. Clive Wilson obtained a High Court order instructing the defence ministry to produce Chavunduka. Two further High Court orders were issued, but all were ignored. "The judge cannot direct us," said the permanent secretary, Job Whabira. "We will move at our own pace." When told that the military had no right to arrest civilians, Whabira replied: "Any civilian who meddles in military matters is subject to military law." It was only when the High Court threatened to issue a warrant for the arrest of the defence minister, Mahachi, that the army finally handed Chavunduka over to the police after eight days, before taking him back to the barracks to be tortured again.

On January 21, the two journalists appeared in a magistrate's court charged under the Law and Order (Maintenance) Act with publishing false reports "likely to cause alarm, fear or despondency to the public." Released on bail, they described their ordeal of torture in the barracks, showing cuts, bruises, and electrode marks. Their allegations of torture were confirmed by medical examiners. Their employer, Clive Wilson, described their treatment as "absolutely disgraceful, like something out of Nazi Germany."

Mahachi called the reporters "liars who had injured themselves." The home affairs minister, Dumiso Dabengwa, threatened to introduce new laws to protect the military against "bad press." And the police arrested Clive Wilson, holding him over a weekend without charging him.

The government's clear contempt of the courts and its use of torture and arbitrary arrest provoked a torrent of international condemnation. In an unprecedented move, the European Union and seven donor governments issued protest notes. A group of about 150 lawyers and human rights activists demonstrated outside parliament, demanding an end to state torture and protesting against the use of the Law and Order (Maintenance) Act. They were dispersed by riot police with batons, dogs, and tear gas.

The most serious rebuke, however, came from judges of the Supreme Court. In a five-page letter to Mugabe, which was passed to the press for publication, they warned that the illegal detention, interrogation, and torture of the two journalists had serious ramifications for the rule of law in Zimbabwe. Two of the judges who signed the letter were black; one was white; two other Supreme Court judges were abroad at the time but endorsed their colleagues' statement. Their petition to Mugabe was also supported by a High Court judge, acting on behalf of fellow High Court judges.

> What is of great consequence is the public perception that the army and/or the CIO can operate with impunity in breach of the law. No minister or senior army officer or senior officer of the CIO has come out with any firm statement in defence of the rule of law. Nor has the Commissioner of Police issued any statement to reassure the public that he and his officers would not allow themselves to be overruled and manipulated in their own sphere of authority in law enforcement.
>
> None of them has appeared before the courts to explain or justify what they or their officials are said to have done or not done. It has never, apparently, been possible to serve on them any of the court orders that have been made, and the impression has been created that those concerned are playing cat and mouse with the courts.
>
> Equally serious is the allegation that the police are either unwilling or unable to prevent the army and/ or the CIO from breaking the law....
>
> Unless the rule of law is firmly established and recognised to be so by the people of Zimbabwe and the international community, it becomes difficult if not impossible for the judiciary to function. It is for this reason that we have approached you today. If the judiciary is ignored, or seen to be ineffective, then anarchy prevails.

The judges set out six points relating to the rule of law on which they wanted Mugabe to give public reassurance. They asked for

TOP: War veteran-led land invaders peg out land and put up signs to turn away outsiders during the spate of land occupations that started in January 2000. This sign is outside *Parklands* farm in the Norton District 50km south of Harare.
*(AP Photo/Rob Cooper)*

BOTTOM: Movement for Democratic Change supporters march through Kwekwe, between Bulawayo and Harare.
*(PictureNET Africa/Henner Frankenfeld)*

LEFT: A pregnant and injured woman is helped by a fellow worker after she fell, while trying to escape war veterans on 24 April 2000, on the farm *Dean* in the Hwedza district 150 km east of Harare.
*(AP Photo/Karel Prinsloo/Sunday Times)*

BELOW: Joan Tapson surveys the gutted lounge of the homestead on her son Russel Tapson's farm *Dean* in the Hwedza district 150 km east of capital Harare, after war veterans set fire to the house and a tobacco barn.
*(AP Photo/Karel Prinsloo/Sunday Times)*

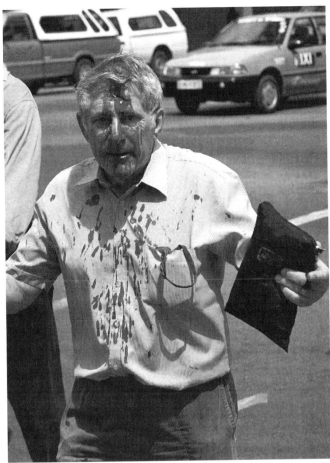

LEFT: During a protest march in Harare organised by the National Constitutional Assembly on 1 April 2000, this unidentified man was severely beaten by a war veteran.
*(AP Photo/Rob Cooper)*

BELOW: War veterans stop a vehicle belonging to Ian Smith, near his farm outside Bulawayo, 16 May 2000.
*(AP Photo/Schalk van Zuydam)*

TOP: Although several farmers were killed during the land occupations, farmworkers bore the brunt of Zanu-PF and war veteran wrath. Here a group from *Barrymore* farm near Virginia, 150km from Harare are driven to the police station to report the burning down of their dwellings on 1 October 2001. *(AP Photo/str)*

BOTTOM: Cartoon published in *Sunday Ti* Johannesburg on 19 August 2001.

THE MOMENT ARRIVES WHEN SOUTH AFRICA DECIDES IT'S TIME TO SAY SOMETHING...

statements repudiating the use of torture, declaring that the military had no right to arrest or detain civilians, and committing the government to investigate the actions of the army in illegally arresting the two journalists.

Mugabe remained silent throughout the furore. He had been on holiday for four weeks, briefly returned for a cabinet meeting, then went abroad. He was said to be aware of how unpopular he had become. A family friend visiting him at his home in Zvimba found him morose. "I've been expecting a bullet," Mugabe told him. But his instinct under adversity was to hit back, to fight to preserve his power, whatever the cost.

On February 6, 1999, he hit back. In a rare address to the nation, he ignored the matter of the journalists' illegal arrest and torture and implied that they had got what they deserved. "If the *Standard* had not behaved in such a blatantly dishonest and unethical manner the army would not have acted in the way it did. Any media organisation which wilfully suspends truth necessarily forfeits its right to inform and must not cry foul when extraordinary reaction visits them." The army had naturally been shocked and angered at the report that had been published. "Propelled by their unquestionable loyalty and commitment to the defence and security of the State, they went to the source of the falsehood and arrested those who had manufactured it. They had through their own deliberate treasonable act invited that reaction."

Similarly, Mugabe ignored the fundamental issues raised by the Supreme Court judges. The judiciary, he said, had no right whatsoever to give "instructions" to the president on any matter. "Their having done so can clearly be interpreted as an action of utter judicial indiscretion or as one of imprudence or, as I regard it, an outrageous and deliberate act of impudence." The judges, he said, had brought into question their own integrity. "If judges assume both a judicial and quasi-political role, what suffers is in effect their judicial function. In those circumstances the one and only honourable course open to them is that of quitting the bench and joining the political forum."

Next Mugabe turned his attack on whites. The peace and stability that Zimbabwe enjoyed, he said, were being undermined "by the acts of some white persons of British extraction who have been planted in our midst to undertake acts of sabotage aimed at affecting the loyalty not just of people in general but also that of the vital arms of Government like the army, so that these can turn against the legitimate Government of this country."

He singled out by name several prominent figures. Two were newspaper executives, Clive Wilson and Clive Murphy; one was an outspoken lawyer, David Coltart; and one was the chairman of the Catholic Commission for Justice and Peace, Mike Auret, a tireless campaigner for human rights since Rhodesian days:

> The likes of Clive Wilson and Clive Murphy, complemented by the Aurets and Coltarts of our society, are bent on ruining the national unity and loyalty of our people and their institutions. But we will ensure that they do not ever succeed in the evil machination. Let me state this and quite emphatically: they have pushed our sense of racial tolerance to the limit.
>
> Let them be warned, therefore, that unless their insidious acts of sabotage immediately cease, my Government will be compelled to take very stern measures against them and those who have elected to be their puppets.

By attacking the judiciary, the press, and human rights activists on such spurious grounds, Mugabe exposed to full public view the truly menacing nature of his regime. There was no longer any pretence that the government possessed a coherent strategy or sense of direction. Mugabe made no attempt to deal with any of the calamitous economic and social issues facing his government. All that mattered to him was the exercise of power.

Two weeks later, in a television interview to mark his seventy-fifth birthday, Mugabe delivered another tirade, lashing out at all and sundry, a paranoid ruler obsessed by plots against his government. Almost as soon as the interview started, he began a sustained attack on whites. The political situation in the country, he said, was "good, in respect of the black community"; but whites were "trying to live in the Rhodesian past." He claimed that "there is a lot of clandestine activity by the white Rhodesian establishment across the world." He accused Western embassies in Harare of acting as "agents for subverting my government," by providing assistance to the increasingly influential labour movement. He dismissed his black critics as "black white men wearing the master's cap." And he renewed his attack on the judiciary, describing the four judges who had signed the petition as "the gang of four" and suggesting they should "pack up and go" as he no longer had confidence in them. He refused to discuss the issue of his retirement, but indicated that he was far from ready to stand down. "Three years I have done, three years to go," he said, referring to his six-year presidential term. "When the moment comes close, I will give my party notice."

The judges, however, proved far more resilient than Mugabe expected. Meeting to discuss how to deal with Mugabe's threats, all twenty-five Supreme Court and High Court judges, seventeen of them non-white, were adamant that they would stand firm. The chief justice, Anthony Gubbay, spoke openly of the need for Zimbabweans to uphold human rights "to prevent community disharmony, civil strife and anarchy." Nor did Mugabe have the power to dismiss them. When this was pointed out to him during his birthday television interview, he appeared to be taken by surprise. "We have not looked into that," he said.

The courts also acted decisively in disposing of the charges against the two journalists. In a landmark judgement in a case brought by the *Standard* challenging the constitutionality of the section of the Law and Order (Maintenance) Act under which

Chavunduka and Choto had been charged, the Supreme Court
ruled that it contravened the section of the constitution allowing
freedom of expression and dismissed the charges.

Chavunduka and Choto then lodged civil and criminal com-
plaints with the commissioner of police, Augustine Chihuri, against
the police and the army, seeking redress for their torture ordeal.
Their claims against the police were based on the incident in which
the police had handed them over to the army, thus facilitating their
torture. Chavunduka furnished the police with information about
the identity of the torturers and told them he was willing to identify
the culprits at an identity parade. When the police took no action,
the two journalists applied to the courts for assistance. The chief
justice, Anthony Gubbay, ordered Chihuri to make a full investigation into the charges of torture and unlawful detention and to prosecute suspects. "It is with regret that I find that the commissioner of
police has failed to afford the applicants the protection of the law
they are entitled to expect from him." Chihuri took no action.

In dealing with his foreign critics, Mugabe adopted the same
hectoring manner. When the International Monetary Fund withheld loans from Zimbabwe, citing its military spending in the
Congo, its forced redistribution of land, and many aspects of its
economic policy, Mugabe claimed the IMF was "bent on stifling development in the third world." Returning to Harare in May 1999
from a fifteen-day trip to China, Singapore, Iran, and the United
Arab Emirates, Mugabe declared: "I do not like the IMF. It is a tool
being used by the western imperialists to subject us to their will.
The IMF is being political and we will be political in our attitude
towards it. It is a monster we do not deserve. We are better off without it. We will be happy without it. We will not die as a country.
Never ever."

By contrast, he praised China, which had pledged to provide
some soft loans. "Of all the countries, China has been our strongest

supporter," he said. "If we get funds from China the way we expect, as per their promises, there will not be any need for us to look for balance of payments support elsewhere." Harking back to the guerrilla war twenty years before, he recalled China's support for Zanu-PF at the time, describing China as "the greatest of friends." Not so the Europeans, he said. "No European country gave us weapons. We were seen in places such as London as the wrongdoers and we were called terrorists because we were fighting the white man. To this day we are still being called terrorists.

"Despite what they say about human rights, the Europeans are the most racist people, racist to the core.... For all their appearances of being democratic, you just have to go to the United States to see how blacks live."

Mugabe's refusal to adhere to IMF conditions lost him the support of both the IMF and the World Bank. Western governments, too, increasingly spurned Zimbabwe, tired of the corruption, mismanagement, and human rights abuses for which Mugabe's regime was now renowned. Britain, under its new Labour government, took a notably harder line than before. "We will not support corrupt governments, we will not subsidise economic mismanagement," said Peter Hain, a British minister. "We will not fund repression or bankroll dictatorship."

Relations between Britain and Zimbabwe descended into farce in October 1999 when Mugabe, on a private visit to London, was accosted by a gay rights activist who tried to effect a citizen's arrest. As Mugabe was leaving St. James's Court Hotel in Buckingham Gate in a mini-cavalcade to go shopping at Harrods, his car was surrounded by gay rights protesters. One of them, Peter Tatchell, opened the car door, grabbed Mugabe by the arm, and said: "President Mugabe, you are under arrest for torture. Torture is a crime under international law." Turning to Mugabe's security officers, Tatchell told them: "Call the police. The president is under arrest on charges of torture." He then remonstrated with Mugabe, citing the torture of Choto and Chavunduka, before the police intervened.

Smarting from such humiliating treatment, Mugabe described Tony Blair's government as "little men" and accused it of using "gay gangsters" against him.

# [10]

## *CHINJA MAITIRO!*

AFTER SO MANY years of mismanagement and plunder, the signs of decay and disintegration in Zimbabwe were everywhere. Harare once boasted of being the cleanest city in sub-Saharan Africa, but it had long since lost all its lustre. It was more noted now for debris on the sidewalks, cracked cement pavings, broken street lights, potholes, uncollected refuse, and burst pipelines. A new executive mayor, Solomon Tawengwa, took office in 1995 promising to eradicate corruption and financial indiscipline and to wipe out the housing waiting list of 100,000 people in three years. But his most notable accomplishment was to build a new mayoral mansion for Z $65 million. As well as being provided with an official Mercedes-Benz, he demanded an expensive four-wheel drive vehicle so he could "access remoter parts of the city." By the time he was suspended for gross mismanagement in 1999, the city's finances were in an even worse mess and the housing backlog had doubled. More than half the population lived in backyard shacks and squatter settlements in insanitary conditions, posing a serious public health threat. The public transport system was decrepit. Street crime was endemic. And the municipality, struggling with ageing equipment, shrinking budgets, and low staff morale, was a spent force.

Harare's main public hospital, Parirenyatwa, once one of the finest health institutions in southern Africa, was regarded as little more than a death trap, shunned by patients whenever possible. Only a few of its operating theatres were useable. There were serious shortages of drugs and equipment, of bed linen, of protective clothing, of food. Its buildings were dilapidated, with leaking roofs, rusting pipes, and broken toilets. Obsolete equipment lined the corridors. Qualified staff departed for positions abroad in ever-increasing numbers.

Other public services were in similar straits. The police were renowned for incompetence and corruption. Even the police commissioner, Augustine Chihuri, was prepared to admit that corruption was widespread and deep rooted. The government-controlled newspaper, the *Sunday Mail*, published an article in September 1999 deploring the deteriorating standards of the police. Calls to the police, said the newspaper, often went unanswered. The article related how one Harare resident, after being mugged in the street, managed to get through to a police "hotline" but was then passed from one office to the next. "The more unfortunate ones are ordered to do the impossible—'Bring the assailant to the police station.' Or one is greeted with a series of questions. Do you know the person who broke into your house? Who do you think did it? Where were you when your house was broken into? And, please come to the station tomorrow because we do not have transport at the moment!"

The Zimbabwe Electricity Supply Authority (Zesa) declared in February 1999 that it was technically insolvent, crippled by government-imposed controls and mounting foreign debt. A subsequent parliamentary inquiry into Zesa reported that it was so permeated with intrigue, insubordination, and "entrenched corruption" that corporate governance had virtually collapsed. The corporation had lost nearly Z $10 million through theft and fraud by senior personnel still working for it.

Even worse examples of corruption were rife within the state oil distribution company, Noczim. In February 1999 the government was obliged to suspend the entire management after finding that managers had siphoned off an estimated Z $1.5 billion over five years. With an accumulated debt of Z $9 billion, Noczim struggled to find funds to pay for oil imports. In December 1999, after suppliers turned off the tap, Zimbabwe was gripped by a critical fuel shortage that affected every sector of the economy. Motorists were obliged to spend hours queuing in long lines outside petrol stations in the hope of obtaining small amounts of fuel. There was also an acute shortage of paraffin, used by the urban poor for cooking. With foreign currency reserves exhausted, the government was forced to seek loans from the few friends it still possessed, such as Libya. Mugabe made a personal visit to Kuwait hoping to obtain lines of credit for fuel supplies, but his trip ended in failure. For the first time since independence, Zimbabwe began to default on its debt repayments.

The plight of the ordinary population, now numbering 13 million, was increasingly desperate. At the end of the 1990s they were 10 percent poorer on average than at the beginning. More than 70 percent lived in abject poverty. The value of wages in real terms had fallen during the decade by 22 percent. No more than 25,000 new jobs a year had been created in the formal sector, one-tenth the number of pupils leaving school each year. The unemployment rate had risen to about 50 percent. Inflation was reaching 60 percent. Output was falling in the mining and manufacturing sector. The government's spending on education amounted to only Z $6 a year for each child enrolled in school. Life expectancy, because of AIDS, had fallen from an average of 52 years in 1990 to 41 years in 2000.

The popular mood was reflected in the songs of Thomas Mapfumo, one of the country's most renowned musicians. During

Rhodesian days, his *"Chimurenga"* songs had been banned from broadcasting and he himself had been arrested and detained without trial for ninety days. At independence he had been a keen supporter of Zanu-PF; his songs were praised by Mugabe. But he had eventually tired of the greed and corruption of the chefs. His popular 1990 album, *Chamunora* (Corruption), was duly banned from broadcasting. In a new album he released in 1999, *Chimurenga Explosion*, his songs questioned the government's involvement in the Congo when people were dying in hospital from lack of drugs and spoke of "the beautiful country that Mugabe has turned to hell." His songs were banned from the state media, and facing harassment, he went into exile to the United States. "Zimbabwe was no longer safe for me and my family," he said.

As the economic crisis deepened, Tsvangirai's labour movement flexed its muscles, organising a series of protest strikes aimed at forcing the government to change course. Mugabe responded by issuing a decree under the Presidential Powers (Temporary Measures) Act banning national strikes for six months. He threatened to suspend the registration of any trade union defying the decree and to imprison its organisers. The CIO was sent to investigate the ZCTU's source of funds.

But Tsvangirai remained undaunted. As well as using the unions in his struggle against Mugabe, he threw his weight behind a wider alliance of civic organisations, church organisations and groups representing human rights activists, lawyers and journalists that had linked up to campaign for constitutional reform. In 1998 they launched the National Constitutional Assembly (NCA), with Tsvangirai as president, seeking public support for a new constitution. They were determined that the process of constitutional reform should be kept on a non-partisan and transparent basis, free from manipulation by Mugabe. They specifically wanted electoral reform in place by the time of the next parliamentary elections, due in 2000. Workshops and consultations were held in towns across the country.

In addition to supporting the work of the NCA, Tsvangirai's ZCTU and members of some thirty civic groups decided at a convention in February 1999 to form a new political party to challenge Zanu-PF at the 2000 elections. The Movement for Democratic Change (MDC) was launched in September, with Tsvangirai as its leader. Its slogan was *"Chinja maitiro!"* — "Change the way you are doing things!"

Mugabe decided that the best way to counter the activities of the NCA was to initiate his own exercise for constitutional reform. In April 1999 the government set up a Constitutional Commission, which was given the task of drawing up a new constitution to be put before the electorate in a national referendum. The Constitutional Commission was dominated by Zanu-PF. Most of its 400 members were Mugabe's nominees from Zanu-PF, including all 147 members of parliament. About one-quarter were considered to be "independent." In August, teams of commissioners fanned out across the country, holding meetings to gather the electorate's views.

Seeing its project hijacked, the NCA urged the public to boycott the Constitutional Commission. The MDC also spurned the Constitutional Commission, calling instead for the creation of a "people's constitution" that would promote accountability and open government.

The Constitutional Commission released its draft constitution in November. It proposed a number of important reforms, including "independent" commissions on public expenditure, elections, corruption, and the media; but it left the vast powers and patronage that Mugabe had acquired as president over twenty years untouched. Although the draft proposed that the president would in future be restricted to two terms of five years, this was not to apply retrospectively, leaving Mugabe with the right to hold office for an additional ten years.

During the commission's final debate, independent members repeatedly pressed for a clause that would stop Mugabe from standing for reelection to the presidency for a third term. But their objections were overruled by the chairman, Judge Godfrey Chidyausiku, who insisted that transitional arrangements fell outside the commission's remit. To the accompaniment of cries of "no," Chidyausiku declared the draft adopted by "acclamation," and the commissioners duly trooped off to present it to Mugabe at a special ceremony at State House.

Without consulting the Constitutional Commission, Mugabe added his own twist to the draft constitution. By special gazette, he inserted an amendment allowing land expropriation without consultation, believing that it would help secure the rural vote. The amendment declared that Britain, as the former colonial power, was responsible for the payment of compensation for land seized. If Britain defaulted, said the amendment, then "the government of Zimbabwe has no obligation to pay compensation."

The MDC pointed out the absurdity of the amendment. "We have no legal authority to compel the British government to do anything," said the MDC's spokesman, Professor Welshman Ncube, a constitutional lawyer. "These are slogans. This is not a constitution." The Commercial Farmers Union made clear their opposition to the draft constitution, mobilising the white farming community against it.

The referendum campaign during January and February 2000, coming at a time of mass unemployment, rising poverty, fuel shortages, factory closures, power cuts, crumbling public services, corruption scandals, and an unpopular war in the Congo, focused as much on the government's record as on the draft constitution. Mugabe blamed the economic crisis on farmers and industrialists, on hoarders and speculators, on Britain, and on the IMF and the World Bank, and stirred up anti-white sentiment. Government-controlled newspapers, the radio, and television followed suit. "While 20 years ago we fought [the whites] using AK rifles, today we are using a pen and ballot paper," said the *Sunday Mail*. "But the war is no less important than in the 1970s. The enemy is the same." Whites were said to be the masterminds behind the MDC, using it to protect their own interests. They were warned that if they encouraged their employees to vote "no" they would face repercussions.

The Constitutional Commission, abandoning any pretence at impartiality, used the same crude tactics, accusing whites of conspiring with Britain to defeat the popular will. "The same white settlers, with the help of the British Government and their international friends, are funding sellout Zimbabweans to buy your rights by urging you to vote 'no,' it claimed. Day after day, the propaganda blitz continued.

Allowed virtually no access to the government-controlled media, the MDC and NCA concentrated their efforts on public meetings, attacking the draft constitution for giving the president too much power and patronage and failing to provide enough checks and balances. White activists played a significant part in the campaign. Although there were incidents of violence, the referendum campaign was notable for the extent of open political activity that occurred.

The result was a stunning defeat for Mugabe. The draft constitution was rejected by 55 percent of the voters. The turnout was low. Only one-quarter of the electorate voted: 1,312,738 out of a potential electorate of 5 million. Most of the "no" votes came from urban blacks: 60 percent were cast in the main centres of Harare, Bulawayo, and Mutare and six other provincial towns. Rural voters—the traditional power base of Zanu-PF—largely abstained, despite promises of land. The result shook Zanu-PF to the core.

Mugabe initially put a brave face on the defeat. Looking tired and holding a script with a visibly shaking hand, in a television address he described the result as "unfortunate" but declared, "Let us all accept the verdict and plan the way forward." He congratulated the electorate on the peaceful nature of the referendum:

Especially remarkable was the rare sense of order, maturity and tolerance during the process. The world now knows Zimbabwe as that country where opposing views can file so singly and so peacefully to and from the booth without incident. I have every confidence that the forthcoming general elections will be just as orderly, peaceful and dignified. May I also make special mention of the white part of our community who this time around sloughed off apathy to participate vigorously in the whole poll.

These fine words, however, concealed an inner rage at what had happened. Mugabe attributed his defeat principally to the whites and was determined to make them pay for it. At an emergency meeting of Zanu-PF's central committee on February 18, three days after the results of the referendum were announced, there were recriminations all round. The ruling elite had suddenly seen their grip on power slipping and with it all the wealth, the salaries, the perks, contracts, commissions, and scams they had enjoyed for twenty years. Some members thought Mugabe had become an electoral liability and bluntly told him he should step down before the forthcoming election. Mugabe in turn blamed his colleagues for failing to fight an effective campaign. All were agreed, however, that what was needed was a far more aggressive election campaign.

# [11]

# THE INVASIONS

IN A CAREFULLY coordinated campaign starting on February 26, 2000, gangs armed with axes and pangas invaded white-owned farms across the country. Government and army trucks were used to transport them to the farms and to keep them supplied with rations once there. They were called war veterans, but the majority were too young to have participated in the war twenty years earlier. Large numbers were unemployed youths paid a daily allowance. Their immediate task was to peg out plots of land. But the wider purpose of their deployment was to crush support for the opposition in rural areas in the run-up to the election.

The land invasions had a devastating impact on the white farming community. The owner of a Marondera farm, Cathy Buckle, kept a record of the disruption and terror the invaders caused and of the tragic outcome, sending regular dispatches to a local independent newspaper. Like many white farmers, the Buckles had bought their 1,000-acre farm after independence. In accordance with government regulations, they had obtained a certificate declaring that the government had no interest in the property. For ten years they had put their hearts into it, developing herds of cattle and sheep, planting gum trees, running a small dairy and trading store, stocking dams with fish, and struggling to pay off debts.

Rumours that Stow Farm was to be invaded left Cathy Buckle shaking and sobbing in disbelief. Her initial reaction was to flee, but after taking precautions to send her seven-year-old son away from home, she decided to stay, waiting in fear and trepidation.

The first she knew of their arrival on March 4 was when her storekeeper, Jane, came running through the gum trees screaming: "They're coming, they're coming. Hide yourself, they're coming." Cathy ran to the house, locking the gates. In the distance she could hear the invaders singing war songs and whistling, one voice shouting above the rest: "Hondo! Hondo! Hondo!"—chiShona for war.

A group of men wearing dark blue overalls came to the gate, calling for Cathy to come out. In the fields below, others began to peg out plots of land. They left later that day, but returned a week later to build a permanent camp, hacking down trees and bringing cattle with them. The police refused to intervene. A large blue tent was pitched a hundred yards from the farmhouse, enabling the invaders to watch every move the Buckles made.

In a dispatch to the local newspaper, Cathy Buckle wrote: "Two small earth dams are now in 'liberated land' and I can no longer water my livestock. I have had to move all my cattle and probably only have enough grazing for another three or four weeks.... When is enough, enough? Can any of us, town and country alike, ever feel safe again when the police refuse to act? I don't know about you, but I'm ashamed to be a Zimbabwean at the moment."

This was but the beginning of the ordeal.

By March 8 nearly 400 farms had been invaded. Some groups merely caused disruption; others were more aggressive, threatening violence, slaughtering cattle, demanding transport, and breaking into farmhouses. The police commissioner, Augustine Chihuri, an ex-combatant himself, claimed there was nothing the police could do to stop the invasions. "It is a political issue," he said. "What do you expect the police to do? ... Talk to the politicians about it."

Mugabe's initial pretence was that the land invasions were a spontaneous uprising by land-hungry peasants denied access to land by rich white farmers. But it soon became evident not only that the invaders were being paid but that prominent Zanu-PF officials, army officers, CIO agents, and even police officers were actively involved in directing events. One of the key figures in the campaign was Perence Shiri, head of the air force and the former commander of 5 Brigade. Mugabe's own colleagues were more straightforward in their explanation. "The whites have themselves to blame because they shot themselves in the foot by mobilising people to throw away the draft constitution," said Didymus Mutasa, a senior Zanu-PF official. "They are now reaping the fruits of their actions."

The government's objectives were spelled out directly by Chenjerai Hunzvi, the war veterans leader whom Mugabe chose to head the campaign. Speaking at Zanu-PF headquarters in Harare on March 15, Hunzvi disclosed that he had been given Z $20 million by the party to organise farm invasions and to campaign for Zanu-PF in the forthcoming elections. The land invasions, he said, would deter whites from campaigning against Mugabe as they had done during the referendum campaign. If they persisted, "we will treat them as enemies."

Hunzvi revelled in his new role. He took particular delight in taunting whites with threats of violence, bragging about the nickname "Hitler," which he had chosen for himself. "Do you know why they call me Hitler," he spat at a white farm manager. "It is because I am the biggest terrorist in Zimbabwe. I am the most dangerous man in this country. And you must do what I tell you." He portrayed the land invasions as a revolution that would return the land to its rightful black owners. "All revolutions require violence," said Hunzvi. "No one can stop the revolution we have started."

The air was soon thick with threats of violence. Another war veteran leader, Andrew Ndhlovu, threatened civil war if the MDC won the forthcoming election. The war veterans would never allow the country "to go back to Smith," he said. If that happened, "it means we will go back to the bush. We will declare a military government. ...We will get arms from government armouries. We are a reserve army and we have the right to use the arms to defend the government of Zanu-PF."

Mugabe added his own threats of violence. Speaking in chiShona at the opening ceremony of a Swedish-funded water project in Manicaland, he declared: "Those who try to cause disunity among our people must watch out because death will befall them."

The Commercial Farmers Union (CFU) urged its members to exercise as much restraint as possible and avoid confrontation. On March 17, it obtained a High Court order declaring the land invasions to be illegal and instructing the police to evict the invaders within twenty-four hours. Hunzvi was personally instructed not to encourage, allow, or participate in any invasion.

But the High Court order was ignored. Hunzvi retorted that he would defy it. "We cannot accept the humiliation of being told by a white man to pack our bags and leave our land." The police, claiming it would be dangerous and counterproductive for them to try to enforce the order, took no action. Mugabe, for his part, described the invasions as "demonstrations." What was more important than "the little law of trespass," he said, was the fight for land. The government would not intervene unless there was violence. "If farmers start to be angry and start to be violent," he said on March 28, "then of course they will get that medicine delivered to them. And it can be very, very, very severe."

Amid the rising tension, the British government raised the temperature further, indulging in a war of words with Mugabe, believing that tough talk was what was required. Peter Hain, an ambitious junior Foreign Office minister, suggested that Mugabe had lost touch with reality. "We have had outbursts from the president that bear little or no resemblance to reality," he said. He portrayed Zimbabwe as a country close to collapse. "Zimbabwe could well fall over the edge of the abyss." He talked openly of Britain's contingency plans for an evacuation of its 20,000 nationals in Zimbabwe, adding to the sense of alarm and fear spreading through the white community. On Stow Farm, Cathy Buckle recorded: "Scary news on the satellite TV this afternoon—Peter Hain said that UK had prepared to accept 20,000 white Zimbabweans—they obviously also think this is getting out of hand."

Hain's interventions served only to enrage Mugabe. They also enabled him to depict the crisis as a struggle by Zimbabwe to gain its rightful heritage against a former colonial power acting on behalf of the white community to protect their interests. The British government, he claimed, was plotting to overthrow him to achieve its aims.

To force the land issue further, Mugabe instructed parliament to pass an amendment to the constitution empowering the government to take over white-owned farms without compensation—the same measure he had inserted into the draft constitution. The amendment declared that "the former colonial power has an obligation to pay compensation for agricultural land compulsorily acquired for resettlement. If the colonial power fails to pay compensation, the Government of Zimbabwe has no obligation to pay compensation for agricultural land compulsorily acquired for resettlement." On the day after the constitutional amendment was passed by parliament, Mugabe told party supporters that if any white farmers resisted the takeover of their land he would not flinch: "Then I will declare the fight to be on and it will be a fight to the finish I can tell you and they won't win the fight, we will win it."

The government also attempted to get the High Court to reverse its order directing the police to evict the land invaders. The attorney general, Patrick Chinamasa, argued in court that police intervention would result in a "bloody confrontation." Delivering his verdict on April 13, Judge Moses Chinhengo upheld the previous order. "The farm invasions are illegal," he said. "The police commissioner therefore had a clear public duty to enforce the order of the court, remove the illegal occupiers and give the affected farmers the protection of the law." He called on Mugabe "to recognise that it is in the permanent interest of Zimbabwe and the rule of law to bring an end to the farm invasions."

Mugabe once more shrugged off the High Court order. Returning from a visit to Cuba, he said on arrival: "I know there is an expectation that I will say to the war veterans 'Get off the land.' I will not say or do that." Nor would he instruct the police to act. "There is no policeman who is going there. We have said 'no.' If the British have their own police they must send them here. Ours are not going to go there." Hunzvi's response was similarly blunt. "They [the judges] can go to hell. They are part of the system which hanged us when we fought for independence. They think they are above the country's executive president. Who do they think we are?"

In April, with the approach of the election, the campaign became increasingly violent. A peace march in the centre of Harare on April 1, organised by civic groups, church organisations, lawyers, and NCA supporters, was attacked by a group of war veterans, led by Hunzvi, who stormed out of Zanu-PF headquarters armed with clubs, barbed wire, and bottles, chanting "Hondo! Hondo!" As the war veterans ran amok, assaulting demonstrators and passersby alike, the police stood by, making no effort to intervene, then fired tear-gas grenades into the fleeing crowd. They made no arrests of war veterans but detained five opposition supporters for disobeying orders to disperse.

On farms under occupation, white farmers faced daily harassment. One Karoi farmer and his family, confronted by an armed gang, were given ten minutes to get off their farm. Another Karoi farmer was punched and whipped in front of his wife until he agreed to sign away half of his farm. A Hwedza farmer, Iain Kay, was kicked, beaten, and marched away with his hands tied with wire by assailants who threatened to kill him; badly injured, he managed to escape by leaping into a farm dam. In Arcturus, the Windrum family escaped from their farm only minutes before an armed mob arrived, looted their homestead, then beat up farm workers and their families, smashing and burning their homes. Another Arcturus couple, David Stobart and his wife, fled after ten truckloads of "veterans" drove up and set fire to their homestead, tobacco barns, and workers' houses. There were similar incidents in Bindura, Mvurwi, Mutepatepa, Marondera, and on the outskirts of Harare.

Farmers known to have helped the MDC in the referendum campaign were singled out for attack. The first victim to be killed, David Stevens, a prominent forty-seven-year-old Macheke farmer, was a local MDC organiser. On April 14 he arranged to take his foreman, Julius Andoche, and a group of his workers to a party rally. On their return to the farm, several workers were beaten up by veterans who had been squatting there for a month. The next day the workers retaliated, chasing them off the farm. The veterans returned later in the morning with a busload of reinforcements.

Stevens tried to negotiate, but the veterans grabbed him, beat him about the head, and tied his hands behind his back with wire. Andoche was also beaten and tied up. The veterans set fire to tobacco barns, looted the homestead, and set off in convoy for Murehwa. Five of Stevens's farming friends, arriving as the convoy was leaving, followed it to Murehwa.

As the convoy approached Zanu-PF headquarters in Murehwa, a veteran leaned out of the window and opened fire on the white farmers. They sought refuge in the police station but, as the police stood by watching, a large group of veterans seized them there and took them to a nearby compound. One farmer, John Osborne, was hauled into a room where he found Stevens and Angoche. All three were beaten, threatened with death, and harangued for not supporting Zanu-PF. Then they were taken into the bush and severely beaten again. Osborne's life was spared by a woman who recognised him and said he should be left alone. Stevens and Angoche were shot dead. The four remaining white farmers were beaten throughout the night and then dumped in the bush, badly injured.

The identities of the veteran leaders who abducted and killed Stevens and Angoche were well known to the police, but they took no action. When one man was eventually arrested, the prosecution case was withdrawn "for want of evidence." The government-controlled radio claimed that it was Stevens who had started the violence. Mugabe concurred. "He was the one who started the war. He was the one who started firing," he said.

Three days later, on April 18, the twentieth anniversary of Zimbabwe's independence, a convoy of thirteen vehicles packed with armed men left Bulawayo at dawn heading for a cattle ranch near Nyamandlovu owned by Martin Olds, a prominent forty-two-year-old white farmer known to be sympathetic to the MDC. Forewarned by reports that the Nyamandlovu district might become a target for veterans, Olds had taken the precaution of sending his wife and two children to Bulawayo.

As the convoy passed through Nyamandlovu on the road to the ranch, police waved it through and then set up a roadblock to prevent others from going the same way. About a hundred men surrounded Olds in his homestead, setting up firing positions. Olds telephoned a neighbour, Guy Parkin, saying the situation looked "pretty serious," then went outside to negotiate. He was hit by a bullet in the leg, but managed to get back inside his house and send out emergency calls, asking for an ambulance. For three hours Olds held off his attackers, crawling from room to room. Guy Parkin tried to reach him but was driven off by gunfire. An ambulance answering Olds's call for assistance was stopped at the police roadblock at Nyamandlovu. A group of white farmers attempting to rescue him was also blocked by police. Finally, after his homestead was set on fire, Olds was forced out into the open and killed. For two hours more the attackers remained at the farm, removing cartridge cases and other evidence, then returned through the police roadblock, waving guns and singing liberation songs.

Olds's murder, carried out by a government death squad in broad daylight with the clear collusion of the police, together with the murder of David Stevens, sent a shockwave through the white community that was never forgotten. White farming families in Matabeleland and in the Macheke district began to flee their farms in droves, seeking the safety of nearby towns. Denied protection and assistance by the police, they were defenceless. The crisis they faced had now passed beyond the issue of land demands. For Olds's attackers had been intent not on seizing his land but on killing him.

Later on April 18 Mugabe made an address to the nation full of anti-white rhetoric, attacking what he called "entrenched colonial attitudes" amongst white commercial farmers. "What we reject is the persistence of vestigial attitudes from the Rhodesian yester-years—attitudes of master race, master colour, master owner and master employer." He blamed white intransigence over land reform for the spate of farm occupations.

At a subsequent news conference, Mugabe went further. Referring to the government's defeat in the referendum, he said: "Their mobilising, actually coercing, their labour force on the farms to support the one position opposed to government, has exposed them as not our friends, but enemies." Making the point even clearer, he went on: "Our present state of mind is that you are now are enemies because you really have behaved as enemies of Zimbabwe. We are full of anger. Our entire community is angry and that is why we now have the war veterans seizing land."

To call white farmers "our enemies" when many were surrounded by armed gangs of vengeful war veterans and two of them had just been killed was tantamount to inciting violence and condoning murder. Even Mugabe realised he had gone too far and later tried to deny making the remarks.

Watching Mugabe on television at Stow Farm, Cathy Buckle wrote: "Zimbabwe's twentieth anniversary of independence would be remembered for a long time. A day of grief and mourning, of pain and bloodshed, of disbelief and despair."

The following day, Mugabe summoned an urgent meeting at State House between farmers and war veterans, representing himself as a "neutral referee." Among those taking part were Chenjerai Hunzvi and Perence Shiri, the former 5 Brigade commander. Mugabe's hope was that the farmers would offer up land to avoid further violence. "What are the farmers prepared to do?" he asked. "What land are they prepared to yield?" Nothing was resolved.

More violence seemed inevitable. On the day after the meeting with Mugabe, the CFU, having received reports that several hundred war veterans were converging on Matabeleland North, ordered the immediate evacuation of all commercial farmers in Matabeleland to Bulawayo. Similar orders went out to Headlands, Hwedza, Virginia, Macheke, Enterprise, and the Midlands. The Marondera district was badly affected, as Cathy Buckle recorded:

> The violence after the murder of Dave Stevens raged down from Macheke—exactly as we had feared—to almost the entire Ruzawi River area, where gangs of 200-strong armed thugs overran a local security company outpost, and the farmers evacuated. Then it came right to the boundaries of Marondera town as gangs rampaged along the North Road, which is fewer than two kilometres from the centre of town. There were horrific beatings and atrocities in workers' compounds and according to eye witnesses the screams could be heard from three kilometres away. From there these gangs moved onto the Bridge Road (about ten kilometres from where we are) and again started their beatings and intimidation in compounds. At that point two of our neighbours left, which leaves now only a couple of farms between them and us and puts us in the front line.

There were rumours that the forthcoming Easter weekend was to be the occasion for mass violence. "Our workers said that they had heard talk that Sunday, Easter Sunday, was the day when whites were going to be killed en masse," wrote Cathy Buckle. "It was, after all, the president of Zimbabwe who had declared us to be enemies of the state."

The government's indifference to attacks on white farmers was succinctly summed up by Hunzvi, after the death toll had risen to four: "Like in any revolution, the path is always bloody, and that is to be expected and hence no-one should raise eyebrows over the death of four white farmers."

There was to be no respite from the fear and terror that Mugabe had spawned. With war veterans now firmly established on bases on white farms throughout the country, Mugabe launched into his election campaign in earnest. Addressing a rally in Bindura district on April 10, he issued what he called "a declaration of war" against the opposition: "The MDC will never form the government of this country, never ever, not in my lifetime or even after I die. *Ndinya kupikirei ndinomuka chidhoma*—I swear my ghost will come after you."

The brunt of this "war" fell most immediately on farm workers and their families living on white-owned farms. Some 400,000 workers were employed by white farmers. Together with their wives, they constituted a sizeable portion of the electorate, as much as 15 percent. To Mugabe they were part of the enemy camp. On one farm after another they were subjected to violence and intimidation by gangs of war veterans acting with impunity. Workers were assaulted, kicked, and whipped; men were abducted, women raped; their homes were destroyed, their property looted. Human rights groups recorded thousands of such incidents.

Several farms, deserted by their owners, were turned into "re-education centres." Using convoys of stolen trucks, tractors, and trailers, war veterans rounded up workers en masse, taking them for indoctrination sessions lasting sometimes for days. Lists of workers said to be MDC supporters were read out before large gatherings, then the individuals named were hustled to the front to be beaten and whipped. For hours on end, workers were forced to chant Zanu-PF slogans and sing "liberation songs." White farmers were sometimes required to attend sessions and join in songs and dances to provide a "good example" to their workers.

Another group singled out for Zanu-PF's attention were teachers, whom government ministers accused of supporting the MDC. Party thugs invaded primary and secondary schools, harassing and abusing teachers, sometimes in front of pupils. Some were beaten; some taken off to "re-education" camps. A teacher at Mutero Mission told a reporter: "The only means to survive is by showing allegiance to the ruling party." Hundreds of teachers in rural areas abandoned their schools and fled to nearby towns for safety. By late May, some 7,000 teachers had deserted, forcing 250 primary and secondary schools to close.

MDC officials and candidates faced acute danger. In April a Zanu-PF gang in Buhera ambushed a car driven by Morgan Tsvangirai's driver, Tichaona Chiminya, setting it on fire; Chiminya and a colleague, Talent Mabika, died from burns. Although their assailants were well-known, no action was taken against them. In Bulawayo an MDC agent, Patrick Nabanyama, was abducted and never seen again, presumed murdered. In the Rushinga district a mob of armed Zanu-PF supporters descended on Nyakatondo village looking for Elliot Pfebve, an MDC candidate, but, failing to find him, they abducted his father and brother; his father was severely injured, his brother killed. Several other attempts were made to kill Pfebve.

In the Chimanimani district a white MDC candidate, Roy Bennett, a prominent local farmer, received a message from Zanu-PF summoning him to a meeting at the country club, along with a warning that he and his family would be killed unless he stood down. Awaiting him at the meeting were the local CIO boss, a police commander, a Zanu-PF chef, two war veterans, and a government official. He was told that he was an enemy of the state and threatened with death, but he emerged from the meeting defiant. "They can take my farm, but I am still running for parliament," he said. "I am having faith in humanity that what the government has done is wrong and the people of Zimbabwe know it and will vote out Zanu-PF and return the rule of law. I am committed. I am not going back. I realise the implications. I realise the threats. I realise the danger. The people of Zimbabwe are being suppressed by a very, very evil regime. I am not going to be intimidated by an evil regime. If I lose my life to it, so be it. For my children to have a life in this country, someone has to make a stand." The next day, Bennett's farm was invaded while he was away. His wife and workers were forced to chant Zanu-PF slogans.

In Kwekwe the MDC candidate, Blessing Chebundo, standing against Emmerson Mnangagwa, endured several murder attempts. His house was burned down. So perilous was his position that he was unable to present his own nomination papers, having to send an election agent on his behalf.

Sporadic violence flared in urban areas between rival groups. In Budiriro, a suburb of Harare, Chenjerai Hunzvi turned his surgery into a base for war veterans, who roamed the area looking for opposition supporters. Victims were brought back to the surgery and tortured. One of them was interviewed by the *Daily News*, a new independent daily newspaper. "About twelve of them picked me up near my friend's shop at about noon," he said. "I had no chance. They said, you are an MDC, and drove me to Hunzvi's surgery. Two others were on the floor naked and bruised. They beat me with electric cables and wooden poles like table legs. They kept shouting, 'Tell us the names of your MDC members.' I kept telling them, I am just a simple man, I am not participating in the party, but they didn't care." Another victim, Takundwa Chipunza, was tortured so badly that he died in hospital. His murder sparked off a spate of re-taliatory violence that left scores of people injured. Only then did the police intervene. Although the police knew full well Hunzvi's involvement in kidnapping and torture, they took no action against him.

The *Daily News* itself was attacked. On April 19 the paper's edi-tor, Geoff Nyarota, received a death threat by letter accusing him of a "lack of respect to our dear president" and of "creating dissatisfac-tion in the government." Three days later a firebomb exploded in an art gallery directly below Nyarota's office on the first floor of a cen-tral Harare building. A CIO assassin was subsequently sent to kill Nyarota but lost his nerve and confessed the plot to journalists. In rural areas such as Murehwa and Shurugwi, war veterans banned copies of the *Daily News* and threatened vendors and truck drivers who tried to deliver them.

At the launch of Zanu-PF's election manifesto on May 3, Mu-gabe made another inflammatory speech, denouncing whites as "sell-outs," branding the MDC as their "puppets," and fulminating against the British government, harking back time and again to the war. "We fought them in a war of liberation to give our people the power to rule themselves, to have democracy—our democracy. In this country there was no democracy, the British never brought the rule of law. Now they think they can teach Mugabe the rule of law." For Britain to try to impose "moral lessons" on his government was a travesty. "We are our own redeemers." As for British whites, "Britain says it will take 20,000 people. They are free to go. We can even assist them by showing them the exit."

Mugabe blamed the outbreak of violence on the MDC. "It is the MDC who started burning houses and shops. They started the vio-lence and now they've got more than they bargained for. We will see to it that peace is there. That's why we have the police force. They want to beat others while they are not being beaten. If you beat a person and that person retaliates, who do you cry with?"

In one election meeting after another, ministers and party candidates used the same threatening language. "We are not happy
with some white commercial farmers who are supporting the opposition," said Josaya Jungwe, the Masvingo provincial governor. "We
do not want another war. If you want peace you should support me
and the ruling party.... If you want trouble then vote for another
party."

Hunzvi was even more direct, telling British whites to leave the
country or face the consequences. "We are now going to search for
those people with British passports.... They must go back to
Britain. They should go to the airport. If they don't, they will go
into the ground."

The small white community in Kariba, a tourist resort by the
lake, was subjected to similar threats by the Zanu-PF candidate,
Isaac MacKenzie. "Let me assure you whites here that once you
support MDC, Zanu-PF is not going to treat you as business people, but as politicians. Then if you are treated as politicians, it is like
signing your own death warrants. The political storm will not spare
you. Let you be informed that our reserve force, the war veterans,
will be set on you."

One rally held in Marondera on May 21 by Mugabe's security
minister, Sidney Sekeramayi, gained particular notoriety. The entire town—businesses, shops, market stalls, and petrol stations—
was forcibly closed down by Zanu-PF youths. Buses were prevented
from leaving the town. Youths went from door to door ordering
residents to attend. Teachers at two schools who declined to go
were assaulted.

About 10,000 people attended the rally. Once there, they were
not allowed to leave. Addressing a group of white farmers and farm
workers who had been required to attend, Sekeramayi commended
them for surrendering their MDC tee shirts. He produced to the
crowd some fifty MDC tee shirts, some of them with bloodstains.
Then he warned: "If we eventually find that you are lying to us, we

shall meet each other. Like we say in the Shona proverb: 'You can't hide from the truth for ever.' After the votes, we will see who has been fooling who and we shall deal with each other."

On Stow Farm, Cathy Buckle watched her workers straggling back to their houses after attending the rally in Marondera:

> I went out to hear their stories. They were hot, thirsty, hungry and exhausted. The buses had taken them to the stadium and then they had sat for the whole day. There was nothing to eat or drink (not for the ordinary people, they said); they were not allowed to leave and when at last the rally had come to an end, there were no buses to bring them home. The 16-kilometre journey back to the farm was a long walk for them but at least they'd been seen attending the rally, they said; at least now they could sleep easy that night. In the tired faces of my workers I saw a reflection of a nation broken, cowed into submission, a people who would do anything to avoid another war. Fear was their ruler.

The handicaps under which the MDC laboured were severe. The MDC reported on June 1, three weeks before the election, that only in twenty-five constituencies was free and safe campaigning possible; in forty-six constituencies campaigning was affected by high levels of intimidation; and in forty-nine constituencies, the level of violence and intimidation was so high that no campaigning was possible at all. "What Mugabe wants," said Tsvangirai, "is to intimidate the whole country into submission." He said the MDC was determined to contest the election even if it meant "playing with ten men."

There was constant pressure from militant activists within the MDC for retaliation. Tsvangirai, reacting angrily to the murder of two supporters, briefly appeared to side with them. "The MDC will no longer sit back and watch our supporters being killed. We cannot stand and watch while our people are being murdered.... We shall devise a strategy to protect ourselves. We shall take this violence to their doorstep. All those engaged in condoning violence, the vice-president, cabinet ministers, MPs, we know who they are. Human life cannot be lost by deliberate action of the state." But he subsequently distanced himself from such sentiments and held the militants in check.

A summary of political violence published in May by the Amani Trust, a human rights group, recorded nineteen deaths: Fifteen were MDC members, supporters, or sympathisers; not one Zanu-PF supporter was killed. The total number of incidents of political violence reported by Amani was 5,070. An assessment of the political affiliations of perpetrators recorded that 86 percent were Zanu-PF supporters and war veterans; 4 percent were MDC supporters.

The predicament of many white farmers became increasingly fraught. By June nearly 1,500 farms had been invaded, and nearly 1,000 of those remained occupied. In three provinces—Mashonaland East, Mashonaland Central, and the northern sector of Mashonaland West—the level of violence and intimidation was severe. Farmers had to contend with more and more demands from war veteran groups—for food, for money, for transport, for fuel, for accommodation—invariably accompanied by threats. Normal farming activity was seriously disrupted. In some cases, veteran groups obstructed the planting of crops, destroyed seed beds, and polluted water supplies.

There was no sign that the crisis would ease. Mugabe was adamant that he would not call off the invasions. Addressing a rally in Gwanda on June 14, he declared: "The court is saying nonsense. It will never happen that blacks should fight each other." He continued: "I will die with my claim to land. My right to land is a right which cannot be compromised. It is our right. It is our land. We must be prepared to die for it."

Hunzvi, summoned before the High Court to explain his repeated defiance of High Court orders, retorted: "It is President Mugabe's prerogative to end the invasions. It is his prerogative that the war veterans are on the farms. He said they could remain on the farms and ordered the police not to evict them. I cannot challenge him."

On Stow Farm, the Buckles were in desperate straits. With much of their grazing land taken over and their funds running low, they were forced to sell prized cattle. "Ten years we had struggled to build up our breeding herd of cattle. Every winter we had scrimped and saved and gone without to buy feed for the cattle," wrote Cathy Buckle. "So many memories, so much hard work." She reasoned that the income would help them survive a few months longer. "Perhaps by the end of September the madness would be over and we could start again." But the Buckles recognised that they were close to losing everything. "For Ian and me, our financial future as farmers was almost finished. We were both middle-aged and had sunk everything we had, and didn't have, into Stow Farm. . . . It broke our hearts to think that we might lose it all for someone's political survival."

Turning the screw further, Mugabe signed a decree under the Presidential Powers (Temporary Measures) Act on May 24 empowering the government to seize farms without paying compensation. A list of some 800 farms and properties to be seized was published in the *Herald* on June 2, the first their owners knew of it. They included large cattle ranches, flower farms, dairy estates, game ranches, tobacco farms, safari properties, abattoirs, and smallholdings. The aim, according to Mugabe, was to ensure an accelerated programme of resettlement, a "fast-track" programme that would enable peasant families to be resettled swiftly. Land would be distributed after the election. The government would meanwhile consider how much more land should be taken. "It is not just the 805 farms that we are now looking at. We are looking at the totality of our land," Mugabe told party candidates on June 7.

> If we allow others to own portions of it, it must be out of our own will, our own desire, our own charity. It will not be on the basis of our colonial history. . . . Perhaps we made a mistake by not finishing

the war in the trenches. We were modest and rushed to Lancaster [House]. If the settlers had been defeated through the barrel of a gun, perhaps we would not be having the same problems. The revolution is yet to be concluded. The next elected parliament should ensure that it concludes this last phase of our revolution. None of us revolutionaries who won the war for independence will want their careers to end without the repossession of our land. Otherwise, what will we tell future generations? The revolution had been fought on the basis that the land will come with political power. What should the fight be about? Our revolution has not ended. We want it to end and the starting point is land.

He said he would not quit politics until the land issue had been completely resolved.

As the violence and intimidation spread, the Catholic archbishop of Bulawayo, Pius Ncube, delivered the most searing indictment of Mugabe that he had ever faced. He spoke of his "violent excesses," blamed him for the lawlessness and disorder that gripped the country, and accused him of trying to divide the country along racial lines. The invasion of white farms, he said, was "illegal and unjustifiable."

Why did the Zimbabwe government embark on such a radical path of land invasions? This was done not to affirm the people. They do not care very much about the people....

The reason...was to revenge against the "No" vote during the constitutional referendum in February and to make sure that Zanu-PF remains in power indefinitely.

The government and Zanu-PF had twenty years to solve the land question and they still had no plan and no commission to tackle the land issue.... Do they care about the people's voice being heard? They definitely do not care about the people's voice—if they did they would have accepted the "No" vote.

Ncube attacked the government's entire record:

> The economy is deteriorating with shortages of fuel and rising prices. People lack food and are unable to afford transport or procure accommodation. Young people are unemployed. Hospital fees are expensive. People lose their houses to auctioneers. The Congo war continues. Destitution grows and misery increases. The decline of the economy is largely owing to corruption and nepotism in the government...This government has been in power for twenty years and the common man is worse off economically.

In Matabeleland, people in rural areas were being forced to buy party cards. They were being threatened with the return of 5 Brigade. "People are defenceless and find themselves like a football being kicked around by the government. The government goes for soft targets, those who are least defended, and terrorises them," Ncube asserted.

The problem, he said, was Mugabe. "He has stayed too long in power and power corrupts. He is completely out of touch."

The response was predictable. Ncube received a number of death threats and a visit from two CIO agents. The CIO, said Ncube after the visit, had been told to put him on a "hit-list" for assassination; the order he believed had come from Mugabe himself.

Long before the election took place, the scale of violence, intimidation, and coercion during the campaign had warped the outcome. In a pre-election report issued on May 22, one month before the election, the National Democratic Institute, a Washington-based organisation, concluded that "conditions for credible democratic elections in Zimbabwe do not exist."

There were particular concerns over the role of Registrar-General Tobaiwa Mudede. A damning verdict on Mudede's reliability was provided by Bishop Peter Hatendi, a former chairman of the Electoral Supervisory Commission, who had resigned in February.

Mudede, he said, had lost all credibility in the eyes of the public and could not be trusted to run a democratic and transparent electoral process. "We want this country to be run on the strength of democratic elections. The process, from start to finish, must be transparent and credible. The body that runs it must be impartial, then it would have integrity and legitimacy. Now, it is important to ask: Is the body credible that is running the current electoral process? The resounding answer we have heard is 'No.'"

True to form, Mudede was as obstructive as ever, deliberately placing administrative obstacles in the way of election monitors, severely undermining their ability to carry out monitoring activity. By prevaricating over the registration of monitors until the day before the election was due to start, Mudede ensured that thousands of monitors were unable to reach outlying districts in time to monitor polling stations there. Opposition parties claimed, moreover, that numerous irregularities had occurred during the registration of voters.

The state media, meanwhile, were used relentlessly to promote Zanu-PF. About 60 percent of the population in rural areas depended on the radio as their sole source of news and information, and they were provided with nothing more than an endless diet of Zanu-PF propaganda. Government-controlled newspapers followed the same line.

In the final weeks before the election, the tide of violence and intimidation abated. With the arrival of hundreds of foreign observers in Zimbabwe, Mugabe was keen to portray the election as a normal democratic occasion. With 30 of 150 seats already in his pocket, he remained confident of retaining a majority in parliament. In any event, his own formidable powers remained untouched. No presidential election was due until 2002.

Voting on June 24 and 25 proceeded in relative calm, but there was a string of incidents involving intimidation and irregularity. In several constituencies, Zanu-PF supporters set up roadblocks to prevent people from reaching polling stations and confiscated their identity cards; independent monitors were ejected from polling stations; there were numerous problems with voter rolls. Overall, however, polling was conducted in an orderly manner.

The result was a narrow victory for Mugabe. Zanu-PF won sixty-two seats, obtaining 48 percent of the votes cast; MDC won fifty-seven seats, obtaining 47 percent. The narrowness of the victory, coming after months of systematic intimidation, was hardly an endorsement of Mugabe's leadership. It was a victory, moreover, which was immediately threatened by the MDC's decision to mount legal challenges in dozens of constituencies where intimidation and irregularities had occurred. The MDC, after only nine months in existence, had won all the seats in Harare and Bulawayo, and ten of the twelve constituencies in Matabeleland; it had also performed strongly in towns in the Midlands and in Manicaland. Zanu-PF was reduced to a party entirely dependent on rural Shona votes; it retained only one urban constituency in the entire country. Without intimidation, Zanu-PF would almost certainly have been defeated.

There were several notable individual results. In Kwekwe Central, Blessing Chebundo, the MDC candidate who had been forced to remain in hiding throughout the campaign, managed to inflict a humiliating defeat on Emmerson Mnangagwa, one of the most feared politicians in the country, known to be favoured by Mugabe as his successor as president. In Chimanimani, Roy Bennett, despite being forced off his farm by war veterans, won his seat. Three other whites standing for the MDC won their seats, including Mike Auret, the human rights campaigner, and David Coltart, the Bulawayo-based lawyer, showing what little impact Mugabe had made by trying to stir up anti-white hostility. Morgan Tsvangirai, who declined a safe seat, lost in Buhera North but successfully contested the result in the courts. Seven Zanu-PF cabinet ministers in all lost their seats. In Marondera East, where there was substantial evidence of electoral fraud, Sidney Sekeramayi hung on with a majority of sixty-one votes. One of the new arrivals in parliament was Chenjerai Hunzvi, elected MP for the Chikomba constituency.

As he had done at the time of the referendum defeat, Mugabe struck a conciliatory note. He called for national unity "across race, tribe, ethnicity, across regions, across class." The election results, he said, "bind us all, loser and winner alike." For a brief period, with the election over, there seemed a chance that the mayhem and destruction might be brought to an end. But it was a forlorn hope.

# [12]

# THE THIRD CHIMURENGA

No sooner had Zimbabwe emerged, battered and bruised, from one election campaign than Mugabe plunged headlong into a new campaign to win the presidential election in 2002. On the pretext that his "revolution" was under threat from an array of forces from both inside and outside the country, he used the police and the army, as well as party militias like the war veterans, to wage war against the opposition, giving them licence to take whatever action they deemed necessary. He called this campaign "the Third Chimurenga," claiming that it would finally set Zimbabwe free from its colonial heritage. But in reality it was no more than a war of violence and intimidation against the electorate to ensure that he retained power.

Explaining the election results to members of Zanu-PF's central committee in July 2000, Mugabe showed the extent to which he was now gripped by paranoia. It would be a serious miscalculation, he said, "to underestimate the forces ranged against us." The MDC was not an ordinary opposition party, as some assumed. It was the manifestation of "the resurgence of white power."

The MDC should never be judged or characterised by its black trade union face; by its youthful student face; by its black suburban junior professionals; never by its rough and violent high-density [urban] elements.

It is much deeper, whiter and wider than these human superficies; for it is immovably and implacably moored in the colonial yesteryear and embraces wittingly or unwittingly the repulsive ideology of return to white settler rule. MDC is as old and as strong as the forces and interests that bore and nurtured it; that converge on and control it; that drive and direct it; indeed that support, sponsor and spur it.

It is a counter-revolutionary Trojan Horse contrived and nurtured by the very inimical forces that enslaved and oppressed our people yesterday.

Among the forces supporting the MDC, Mugabe said, were Britain, the United States, and the old Rhodesian network around the world. "These worked very closely with their kith and kin in MDC and those in the country who stayed behind at independence but who now feel embittered or threatened by our land policy." All had worked to corrupt the election process: "Partisan messages were used in the name of voter education; attempts were made to infiltrate and influence the election supervisory process; pre-election pronouncements were made by organisations of known partisanship, simply to discredit the electoral process in the hope of discrediting the outcome."

White commercial farmers were part of the conspiracy:

Historically, this group has played a controlling role in the country's policies, a role naturally deriving from its position as an economic, political and, until our independence, a military base for white power, its retention and extension.

While at independence this power base of the Rhodesian Front

melted and disguised itself as farming unions or some such group-
ings, it retained its infrastructure and even personnel of guarding
and safeguarding white economic interests in Zimbabwe. This is
the constituency which has created and controlled the MDC....

As we pushed harder for real land reforms, this stratum, which
has always enjoyed a king-making role, began to show its true political colours by exercising its influence over white industrial and
commercial structures, in the process turning shop-floors, farm and
mine compounds into hotbeds of anti-Zanu politics.

This ensured that a broad political front was forged within the
country's farming-industrial-commercial complex, thereby overnight
turning what daily manifested itself as economic power into political
oppositional might; and workers into regimented supporters of the
opposition.

Even the churches, according to Mugabe, were involved:

The most insidious side of the resurgence of white power came by
way of the pulpit and in the human form of church figures who do
not hesitate to "render unto God" things that belonged to Caesar.
Especially in suburban parishes and in rural Matabeleland, prayers
became full-blooded politics and congregations became anti-Zanu-
PF political communities united around hackneyed grievances to
do with the tensions we had before the Unity Accord.

All these forces, said Mugabe, had now started to mobilise for
the 2002 election in the final push to break Zanu-PF's hold on
power. It was the task of Zanu-PF to defeat them.

The police were central to Mugabe's strategy. The police commissioner, Augustine Chihuri, a former war veteran, openly admitted to owing allegiance to Zanu-PF. Under his auspices, the police
were converted into little more than a Zanu-PF militia, harassing
and detaining opposition supporters at will while refusing to touch

Zanu-PF supporters engaged in criminal violence. War veterans and party youths were incorporated into the police, given rapid promotion, and transferred to police stations in rural areas. Victims of political violence reporting to the police ran the risk of a further beating from the police. Selective prosecution became the norm. Officers who tried to maintain professional standards were transferred, demoted, or otherwise victimised.

As a foretaste of what was to come, in the days following the election paramilitary police and soldiers were let loose in the suburbs of Harare, raiding bars and nightclubs where MDC victory celebrations were under way, assaulting patrons and passersby. The official explanation was that they were deployed "to stamp out post-election violence." But the real purpose was to demonstrate what the price was for voting against Mugabe.

Another ominous sign of Mugabe's intentions was his decision to grant an amnesty to the perpetrators of "politically-motivated crimes" committed between January and July 2000, the period covering the land invasions and the election campaign. The main beneficiaries were war veterans and party supporters involved in thousands of incidents of assault, abduction, torture, arson, and property destruction. Crimes such as murder, rape, theft, and possession of arms were not included in the amnesty, but it made little difference because in cases where Zanu-PF supporters were known to be the perpetrators of such crimes, the police took no interest in pursuing them. Some forty opposition supporters were murdered during the election campaign, but even when the police had overwhelming evidence about the identity of the murderers, they were allowed to go free. A murder suspect arrested in connection with the abduction and death of David Stevens, to which there were dozens of witnesses, including the police, was released for "lack of evidence." The killers of Tichaona Chiminya and Talent Mabika were identified by a High Court judge as a CIO officer and a Zanu-PF election agent, but they remained untouched. All this served to encourage Zanu-PF supporters to go on the attack in the knowledge that they could do so with impunity.

The impact of Mugabe's "third Chimurenga" was felt most immediately by the white farming community. As he had signalled during the election campaign, Mugabe moved swiftly to implement his "fast-track" land resettlement programme, extending the number of commercial farms to be expropriated to some 3,000, about two-thirds of the total, covering an area of 12 million acres. Each week a new list of farms designated for expropriation was published in the government press. Farmers were issued with eviction notices giving them thirty days to leave. They were promised payment for "improvements" to their properties at some unspecified date in the future, but nothing for the land, even though many had bought their farms with government approval in the years after independence.

According to Mugabe, the "fast-track" programme was intended to assist the resettlement of landless peasants. But the selection process was controlled by Zanu-PF committees, and it soon became evident that the main beneficiaries were party officials, war veterans, and card-carrying members, many of whom had no background in farming. Farming experience was not a prerequisite for selection. MDC supporters were explicitly banned from receiving any "fast track" land. Moreover, the government had no funds to provide the new settlers with support services or infrastructure. They were taken in government and army trucks to expropriated farms and left to their own devices.

Agricultural experts predicted disaster. Farms that were designated for expropriation included major tobacco, horticultural, and food crop producers. The Commercial Farmers Union calculated that within four years agricultural production would slump by 25 percent. It warned that food shortages, even starvation, would result. Equally serious was the plight of farm workers, numbering some 400,000, who, together with their families, constituted one-sixth of the entire population. The CFU estimated that half of the labour force would lose their jobs, leaving up to a million people destitute.

In addition to the "fast-track" programme, white farmers had to contend with an upsurge in land invasions and harassment by war veteran groups. Farmers were prevented from planting crops, forced to provide food and transport, threatened, abused, and issued with false eviction "orders." Several farming families fled after war veterans occupied their homesteads. "Extortion, destruction of property, theft and threats continue largely unabated on farms," reported the CFU.

One early casualty was the Save Valley Conservancy, a group of former cattle ranches that had joined together to form a huge wildlife area covering 850,000 acres. A thriving tourist destination, the conservancy had imported some 600 elephants and rare species like the black rhinoceros, which had been poached to near extinction in the Zambezi Valley. War veterans moved into the conservancy, shooting and snaring hundreds of animals.

Among other casualties were the Buckles on Stow Farm. They had held out for as long as they could in the hope that conditions after the election would improve. Although their farm was not designated for expropriation by the government as many others in the Marondera district had been, it made no difference. With squatters occupying large parts of their farm, cutting timber, polluting water supplies, ripping down fencing, they were unable to survive. "The farm is littered with plastic, bottles, paper and a dozen or so huts in various states of disrepair," wrote Cathy Buckle. "Five different factions have shouted at us through locked gates. One lot have demanded money and vehicles. One lot have pulled a gun on me and threatened to kill me. One lot started ploughing and burning. One lot burned one of my employees on her upper lip with a hot steel bar."

Finally, the Buckles made the decision to leave. "It seems without doubt that this was the ultimate aim of the 'war veterans'—simply to wear us down, cripple our operations, drive us to the edge of bankruptcy until we gave up. And now they have won."

The land grab became ever more chaotic. Soldiers, policemen, air force officers, war veterans, government officials, party officials, and peasants descended on commercial farms in the thousands in a wild scramble for land as the new rainy season began, building shacks, cutting down trees, hunting down wildlife, and looting abandoned buildings. Farms were occupied whether they were listed or unlisted. Any hint of resistance was dealt with by assaults, death threats, and forced eviction. Party bosses, along with army, air force, and police officers, led the action, taking prize properties for themselves. Driving a Mercedes-Benz and accompanied by a police chief, Mugabe's sister, Sabina, a Zanu-PF member of parliament, led a crusade of war veterans and party supporters into the Norton farming area, urging them to seize white farms at random. One of the country's leading seed maize producers, whose farm had not been designated, lost half of his farm in the scramble.

In an attempt to stop the mayhem, the Commercial Farmers Union launched two actions in the Supreme Court. First, it challenged outright the legality of the entire resettlement programme, arguing that the laws under which the government was acting were unconstitutional; the programme was being carried out unlawfully; and, because of the failure of the police to comply with High Court orders to remove invaders, it was beset by lawlessness. Furthermore, the CFU argued, it was being conducted in a politically and racially discriminatory manner.

While the Supreme Court was considering the issue, the CFU initiated a second action, claiming that the government was failing to comply with legally prescribed procedural requirements in implementing its fast-track programme, such as giving farmers three months' notice to vacate. The Supreme Court dealt first with this second action, declaring in November that the government's fast-track programme was illegal because land seizures were occurring at a time when only preliminary steps in the compulsory seizure process had been taken. Farmers had not been given enough time to appeal against confiscation orders. The Supreme Court accordingly ordered the police to remove all war veterans, squatters, and any others unlawfully occupying farms.

In its judgement on the first action, the Supreme Court ruled in December that the government had also failed to comply with its own laws. While acknowledging the need for land reform, it described the resettlement programme as "entirely haphazard and unlawful." The government had allowed a network of organisations —war veterans, villagers, unemployed urban dwellers—to move on to farms in complete disregard for the law. They had been supported, encouraged, transported, and financed by party officials, government officials, the CIO, and the army. The rule of law had been overthrown in the commercial farming areas, and farmers and farm workers on occupied farms had consistently been deprived of the protection of the law. "Wicked things have been done and continue to be done. They must be stopped. Common law crimes have been and are being committed with impunity."

Furthermore, the Supreme Court ruled, the farm occupations amounted to unfair discrimination. If it had been the case that the government had expropriated farms owned by whites to right historical wrongs, this in itself did not necessarily constitute unfair discrimination on the grounds of race, provided the process was conducted lawfully with payment of fair compensation. But several ministers had announced that only Zanu-PF supporters would be resettled on the land. This amounted to unfair political discrimination. If Zanu-PF officials had been involved in the selection of settlers and the allocation of plots, then the exercise had degenerated from being an historical righting of wrongs into outright discrimination. In conclusion, the Supreme Court insisted that the police restore the rule of law in commercial farming areas and instructed the government to devise a lawful resettlement programme within six months.

By standing firm on the land issue, the Supreme Court became a central target for retribution. But it was not only the land judgements that riled Mugabe. There were other issues that brought the judiciary into collision with his increasingly tyrannical regime, compounding his determination to crush its independence.

One issue concerned the freedom of the media. In September 2000, giving judgement in a case brought by an independent radio operator, Capital Radio, which was seeking permission to start broadcasting, the Supreme Court ruled that the state monopoly on broadcasting was illegal. "There is at present nothing to prevent the applicant from proceeding with immediate effect to operate and provide a broadcasting service from within Zimbabwe," the Supreme Court declared. One week later, Capital Radio began broadcasting music from a small studio in a Harare hotel, the first private radio station in the country. Mugabe's response was to issue a presidential decree imposing new broadcasting laws making it illegal for radio stations to operate without a licence. Fearing reprisals, Capital Radio obtained a High Court injunction after office hours from Judge Ismail Chatikobo barring the police from searching its premises and seizing equipment. Ignoring the injunction, the police raided Capital Radio and the homes of two of its directors. The new minister of information, Jason Moyo, accused the judge of participating in a sinister plot of "night lawyers going to see night judges in a night court to seek night justice." The minister of home affairs, John Nkomo, declared: "The days of going to court will soon be past. We won't accept any resistance."

A more serious collision occurred when Mugabe attempted to prevent the courts from invalidating any of the June election results. Following the election, the MDC mounted challenges in thirty-eight constituencies, nearly one-third of the total, mostly on the grounds of the use of violence, but in some cases because of other irregularities such as bribery. In early December, just one month before the High Court was due to commence its hearings, Mugabe, purporting to act under the terms of the Electoral Act, declared the MDC's petitions invalid and proclaimed the election results would stand. A government spokesman explained: "In a democracy, the consent of the governed to those who govern is so paramount as to require that elections must be decided by the voters themselves and not the courts." He added that the litigation was placing an intolerable burden on the MPs being challenged. However, in response to a petition from the MDC, the Supreme Court unanimously declared Mugabe's action to be unconstitutional.

Striking back, Mugabe unleashed a campaign of vilification against the Supreme Court and the judiciary, using two new ministers to lead the attack. One was Jonathan Moyo, the information minister. A former academic, Moyo had once been a prominent critic of Mugabe's regime, accusing him of "ineffectual leadership," describing his cabinet as "inept" and calling party chefs "puffed-up and fat-headed." But Moyo's academic career had faltered. He was being sued by the Ford Foundation, which had employed him as a programme officer in Kenya, and he also faced demands from South Africa's University of the Witwatersrand for the repayment of fees he had received while on a posting there. Returning to Zimbabwe, he had opportunely thrown in his lot with Mugabe, relishing the chance it gave him to sound off on any subject at Mugabe's behest. In addition to Moyo, Mugabe used Patrick Chinamasa, a lawyer whom he nominated as minister of justice. Neither Moyo nor Chinamasa had any standing in Zanu-PF. They were chosen simply to do Mugabe's bidding.

In November Moyo launched the campaign, accusing the Supreme Court of being biased in favour of white landowners at the expense of the landless majority. Of the five members of the Supreme Court, two were white, two were black, and one was of Asian origin. Moyo singled out for attack the white chief justice,

Anthony Gubbay, a highly respected former Rhodesian judge, born in Britain, whom Mugabe had appointed to the post in 1990. Moyo called on him to resign. Simultaneously, Zanu-PF members of parliament tabled a motion urging Mugabe to set up a tribunal to investigate the conduct of the chief justice and to remove him from office.

Chinamasa then joined in, describing white judges as vestiges of the colonial era. He accused them of stifling the government's land redistribution exercise, claiming they were making racist judgements that favoured whites. "The present composition of the judiciary reflects that the country is in a semi-colonial state, half free, half enslaved. Visitors to our country would be excused from observing, as they often do, that if one came to the country, chaperoned to a sitting of the Supreme Court and made to leave immediately, one would by that fact alone conclude that he had been to a European and not an African country. It is like we have an English court on Zimbabwean soil."

The dominant culture and aspirations in the judiciary were "very much Eurocentric," as it still looked to Europe and America for guidance and inspiration. "Our present judiciary still crave for international acclaim and recognition. . . . Seeking domestic acclaim for judgements delivered does not seem to be of any consequence." This had placed the judiciary on a collision course with the government and earned it a reputation as "the main opposition to the ruling party." Reform of the judiciary was long overdue, Chinamasa said. "We must begin to exorcise from all our institutions the racist ghost of Ian Smith and we do so by phasing out his disciples and sympathisers and fellow travellers. The elements on the present bench associated with the Smith regime must know and be told their continued stay on the bench is no longer at our invitation. Their continued stay is now an albatross around the necks of our population."

On November 24 a more direct threat was made. While the five judges were assembled to hear an application from the Commercial Farmers Union over the land issue, a group of about 200 war veterans invaded the Supreme Court building. They were led by Joseph Chinotimba, a municipal security guard who earlier that morning had appeared in court on a charge of the attempted murder of his neighbour, an MDC supporter. In full view of the police and court officials, the mob poured into the building, waving placards and shouting "Kill the judges." They harassed lawyers representing the CFU, forcing the judges to postpone the hearing for six hours. No one was arrested. Addressing war veterans afterwards outside the Supreme Court, Chinotimba warned that there would be a bloodbath if the land issue was not resolved in their favour. "We went to war because of land," he said. "This is our land and the white judges can go back to their countries if they want to become an obstacle to an equitable land redistribution programme."

Chief Justice Gubbay protested the government's failure to intervene. "Disappointingly, there was no official condemnation of the incident. Not a word was heard from the minister of justice."

The threats against judges became ever more explicit. In December war veterans issued a two-week ultimatum to Supreme Court judges to resign or risk being removed from office. Then they threatened to attack judges in their homes. "We as judges take these threats seriously," Gubbay wrote in a letter to Mugabe. "We are fearful of our safety and the safety of our families. We find it difficult to carry out our onerous judicial duties when placed under pressure of this nature." He appealed to Mugabe to "intervene on the judiciary's behalf and persuade the war veterans to cease their intimidation and leave the judges alone."

It was to no avail. Mugabe was intent not just on ridding the Supreme Court of whites but on leading a new crusade against the entire white community. In a speech laden with crude racist rhetoric, delivered to a Zanu-PF congress in December, just two days after an elderly white farmer had been shot dead at his farm gate,

Mugabe blamed all the country's ills on whites. He denounced white landowners as "white devils," vowing to take all they owned, declaring he was at war with them:

> The courts can do whatever they want, but no judicial decision will stand in our way.... My own position is that we should not even be defending our position in the courts. This country is our country and this land is our land.... They think because they are white they have a divine right to our resources. Not here. The white man is not indigenous to Africa. Africa is for Africans, Zimbabwe is for Zimbabweans.

He accused whites of sabotaging the economy in an attempt to destroy Zanu-PF. The "severe hardships" that the population faced—fuel shortages, unemployment, rising prices—were not caused by government but by whites. "Many people blame us, the government, our party, for all the economic ills that affect our country. But those who control the economy are a racial group. ...They discriminate in every way possible against the majority of the people, they determine how far we can go and what changes are possible.... They are closing their factories and companies in order to worsen our economic condition."

Mugabe's answer to this "onslaught" was to licence terror against whites. "Our party must continue to strike fear in the hearts of the white man, our real enemy," he declared to wild cheers and applause.

The war veterans leader, Hunzvi, was on hand at the party congress to reinforce Mugabe's words: "We are fighting for our land and whosoever is killed, it's tough luck. In fact, it is now going to be very hard for commercial farmers."

As well as white farmers and the judiciary, the independent press came under sustained attack. In January 2001 Zanu-PF supporters in several towns began seizing copies of the *Daily News* and burning them. On January 23 Hunzvi and Chinotimba led a mob of about 500 Zanu-PF supporters through the streets of central Harare to the offices of the *Daily News*, demanding that the paper be banned. Three days later the information minister, Moyo, wrote an article in the *Herald* attacking the editors of the *Daily News*, the weekly *Independent*, and the Sunday *Standard* for being "unpatriotic." He concluded the article with a clear threat: "It is now only a matter of time before Zimbabweans put a final stop to this madness in defence of their cultural interest and national security." On television the next day he was even more explicit: the *Daily News*, he said, would be "silenced."

A few hours later the printing presses of the *Daily News* were destroyed by bombs. The *Daily News* managed to put out a twelve-page edition the following day, but the loss of its own printing presses was a severe handicap. The foreign press too was subjected to harassment. Two foreign journalists were expelled in February, and new regulations were introduced to control foreign media reporting.

The Supreme Court, meanwhile, was struggling to maintain its independence. In January the chief justice, Gubbay, was the target of a stinging attack by the head of the High Court, Godfrey Chidyausiku, a former deputy minister in Mugabe's government who made no secret of his allegiance to Zanu-PF or of his ambition to become chief justice. In an unprecedented move, in November he had attempted to interfere with a Supreme Court ruling that farm occupations were illegal. Now he turned to attacking Gubbay in public, accusing him of bias in favour of white commercial farmers.

On January 22 Gubbay, accompanied by another Supreme Court judge, Wilson Sandura, attended a meeting with Mugabe's vice-president, Simon Muzenda, and two other ministers, anxious to explain the judiciary's mounting concern at the deteriorating state of law and order, including the disruption of court proceed-

ings by war veterans. The meeting turned into an outright vilification of the judiciary. In anger, Gubbay threatened to resign.

This was just the opportunity the government was looking for.
Treating the threat to resign as a formal submission, Chinamasa
called on Gubbay at his chambers to tell him that the government
had accepted his "resignation." If he refused to go, the government
"could not guarantee his safety." At the age of sixty-eight, Gubbay, a
shy, mild-mannered man, with a wife who was seriously ill, could no
longer stand the harassment. Under duress he agreed to take early
retirement and to stand down in June, after he had taken a four-
month period of leave due to him.

Chinamasa next called in two other Supreme Court judges, Nick
McNally and Ahmed Ebrahim, suggesting that they too should take
early retirement, adding the same veiled threat he had made to
Gubbay. McNally recalled: "I was told very politely and very nicely
that I should go—take my leave and go, otherwise anything could
happen. It was said very frankly that they didn't want me to come to
any harm." Ebrahim received the same message. But both decided
to stay. Chinamasa was further thwarted when the remaining
Supreme Court judges, Wilson Sandura and Simbarashe Muche-
chetere, refused to see him.

The campaign of calumny intensified. Zanu-PF's parliamentary
caucus passed a vote of "no confidence" in the Supreme Court and
demanded the removal of all white judges. Moyo argued that "the
very system of our national governance is now under threat" from
the "partial and biased application of the law by the Supreme
Court." Chinamasa told a meeting of the Commonwealth Parliamentary Association, "Judges should represent our interests because if they don't, we will criticise them. They are part of the three
arms of government and if they behave like unguided missiles, I
wish to emphatically state that we will push them out." Mnangagwa,
the speaker of parliament, joined in: "We should guard against the
judiciary developing into an omnipotent entity devoid of any ac-

countability." A prominent Zanu-PF MP, Christopher Mushohwe, claimed in parliament that Gubbay had been "infiltrated into Zimbabwe by British intelligence to overthrow the government" and described him as "a Manchester man with links to very powerful Jewish financial interests."

Determined to clear the way for the appointment of Chidyausiku as the new chief justice, Chinamasa announced in the *Herald* on February 27 that Gubbay's position as chief justice would be terminated on February 28. He would be paid four months' salary in lieu of leave, said Chinamasa, but he would have to vacate his office and his official residence the following day. As from March 1, the government would not recognise any court hearings over which he presided.

Infuriated by this latest manoeuvre, Gubbay stood firm. He issued a statement rejecting Chinamasa's "unlawful demands" and declared that he would remain chief justice, reporting for duty as usual, staying at his official residence and making use of his official car. He added that he would now reconsider the question of his early retirement.

On March 1 Gubbay drove himself to the two-storey Supreme Court building on Union Avenue, hurried past four armed policemen on duty at reception, and walked up the stone spiral staircase to his office on the first floor, staying at work for the rest of the morning. Chinotimba too went to the courthouse, demanding to see Gubbay. He was restrained by officials but vowed to return the next day with supporters. Ignoring the danger, Gubbay drove to his office the next day. Chinotimba arrived and stormed past the police into the Supreme Court but was barred from reaching Gubbay in his office. After making various threats, he settled for talking to Gubbay on a telephone from a downstairs office, threatening him with death unless he left. "He is a British imperialist agent and he must go," Chinotimba told reporters afterwards. "I have told him in no uncertain terms that he is putting his life at risk by remaining in office when we have made it clear we no longer want him. I told him to vacate his office today. If he does not go, we will declare war."

It was an apt symbol of the criminal decrepitude that had overtaken Mugabe's regime that a municipal security guard on trial for the attempted murder of an opposition supporter should walk unhindered into the Supreme Court, threaten to kill the chief justice, then walk out to the applause of the ruling party.

In negotiations with Chinamasa, Gubbay's lawyers reached a truce. It was agreed that Gubbay would retain his position until July 1 but would take immediate leave; that all statements by government ministers impugning Gubbay would be withdrawn; and that no further steps would be taken by the government to remove other judges. In the meantime, an acting chief justice would be installed. The man chosen for the post was Chidyausiku.

Mugabe subsequently confirmed Chidyausiku as the new chief justice. He also expanded the number of judges constituting the Supreme Court from five to eight, appointing three new judges known to support Zanu-PF. Two of them had been granted large cattle ranches at nominal rent. One of Chidyausiku's first actions, sitting in conjunction with the three new judges, was to reverse a previous Supreme Court ruling declaring the government's seizure of white-owned farms to be illegal. "Zimbabwe no longer has an independent judiciary," remarked a defence lawyer involved in the case. "It only has a few independent judges."

# [13]

## REAL MEN

THE TWENTY-FIRST anniversary of Zimbabwe's independence was a grim and gloomy occasion, full of foreboding. Zimbabwe had become a nation bankrupted by mismanagement, corruption, and violence. The economy was in a sharp downward spiral; agricultural production was falling fast, with vast areas of farmland left untended; businesses were closing by the score; the manufacturing sector—clothing, textiles, engineering, the timber trade—was contracting, shedding thousands of jobs; the mining industry was in similar difficulty. The tourism industry—once the rising star of the economy—had virtually collapsed. With a reputation for random violence and anti-white hostility, Zimbabwe no longer attracted foreign tourists. Its tourist capital—the Victoria Falls—had become virtually a ghost town. With no foreign currency reserves left, the government had defaulted on all its foreign loans. The shortage of foreign currency was crippling. Fuel queues formed every day; hospitals ran out of essential drugs. The AIDS pandemic raged unchecked. Three-quarters of the population was officially classified as living in abject poverty.

A growing number of whites, tired of Mugabe's anti-white

tirades and despairing of the economic collapse around them, decided to leave. Mugabe pronounced himself pleased with their departure. The majority of whites in Zimbabwe, he said, were cheats and crooks:

> These crooks we inherited as part of our population. We cannot expect them to have straightened up, to be honest people and an honest community. Yes, some of them are good people, but they remain cheats. They remain dishonest. They remain uncommitted even to the national cause.... We would actually be happier if some country were to accept them, and since Britain said it wanted them to come to Britain, we can open our doors for them, but we will not force anyone out. There are some of them who are good, but I think the bulk of people we would rather do without.

But it was not just whites who were leaving. The exodus included hundreds of black middle-class professionals—doctors, nurses, teachers, and accountants—who saw no future for themselves while Mugabe's regime lasted. Health professionals in particular were frustrated by having to work without drugs and equipment.

In speeches and interviews to mark the anniversary, Mugabe remained as obdurate as ever. He devoted most of his time to attacking Britain over the land issue, resorting to the same old rhetoric he had used year after year. "This land, this Zimbabwe, is a sacred inheritance from our forefathers," he said. "It was the *casus belli* of our armed national liberation struggle. It cannot, therefore, be that which we have to beg a foreign power for and so we say: Hands off, Britain! Hands off, Britain!" He declared that he would remain at his post until the land issue was resolved. And he was adamant that the MDC would never gain power. "There will never come a day when the MDC will rule this country," he said. "Never, ever."

To ensure this outcome, however, he was left with only one option: to use violence. In another phase of "the Third Chimurenga," war veterans and party militias were authorised to broaden their attacks. The army was brought in to retrain war veterans as part of a regular reserve force paid to root out opposition. Hunzvi announced in April 2001 that war veterans would operate not only in rural areas but from "mobilisation bases" in urban constituencies from where they could conduct what he called an "aggressive" presidential election campaign.

Acting as Mugabe's shock troops, just as they had done during the land invasions, war veteran groups stormed into white-owned factories and offices, claiming to represent aggrieved workers. "The way we solved problems on the farms is the same way we are going to solve industrial issues," announced Chinotimba. Operating from Zanu-PF headquarters, war veteran gangs invaded management meetings, ordered the reinstatement of dismissed workers, set up kangaroo courts, assaulted and abducted managers and staff, and seized equipment.

Selecting businesses at random, they invaded a bakery, a transport firm, the head office of a department store, a children's home, a football club, a training centre, a safari company, and a dental surgery. They frog-marched the head of a Harare textile firm five miles to Zanu-PF headquarters and abducted the owners of a game lodge near Harare's international airport, holding them in party offices for four hours. They confiscated twenty-two commuter minibuses belonging to a taxi firm, taking them to Zanu-PF headquarters, stripping them of accessories, then demanding payment for their release. The owners met the police commissioner, Chihuri, asking for help, but Chihuri refused to intervene. They eventually paid $450,000. But even then the war veterans returned to their garage, assaulted mechanics, damaged the premises, and drove off thirty-four minibuses. Fearing for their safety, the owners fled the country.

The gangs invaded a private hospital in Harare, Avenues Clinic, where fifteen operations were under way. The director, Malcolm Boyland, kept a diary of the three-week ordeal he faced before deciding to flee the country:

We had twenty men burst into the office and I was surrounded by yelling men in ugly mood. We had been in a management team meeting one minute and in terror the next. All aggressive and insolent to different degrees. All impatient and very deliberately rude. ...I managed to get the War Vets out of the hospital into the boardroom, away from the patients, in a separate building....We were harangued and threatened. "We will march you to Zanu-PF office and put you in a room with no door."

The police were called but did not come. The war veterans demanded payment over a labour dispute that had occurred six years before, giving a deadline of five hours. Exhausted and fearful of assault, Boyland eventually agreed to pay out $6 million. Day after day the war veterans returned, making new demands. After receiving a telephone call threatening death, Boyland decided to leave.

By May the number of businesses invaded had reached 300, including shops; restaurants; hotels; and the subsidiaries of South African, British, U.S., Australian, Danish, and other foreign companies. Growing ever more ambitious, Hunzvi announced plans to extend the action to foreign embassies and NGOs, which Mugabe regularly accused of assisting the MDC. "Our next target after solving workers' problems in factories and companies will be to deal once and for all with foreign embassies and non-governmental organisations who are funding the MDC," said Hunzvi. "We will be visiting them soon to express our displeasure and to warn them to stop interfering with our internal matters. No one can stop us in our second phase. We will use whatever means we have to deal with these foreign nations here who want to install a puppet regime in Zimbabwe."

Hunzvi's first target was the Friedrich Ebert Foundation, a German NGO involved in civic education programmes. A group of twenty-five war veterans stormed into the Harare office of Felix Schmidt, the director, demanding payment on behalf of two former employees sacked in 1999. "They threatened me. They told me I should come with them to the Zanu-PF provincial offices, where they take people to be beaten up," said Schmidt. The police were called, but refused to intervene. "They said it was not their task to protect me, to chuck them out of my office or arrest them." To avoid further trouble, Schmidt paid up. "The whole thing was extortion," he said.

In Chimanimani, a group of war veterans led a mob of 1,000 villagers in looting a warehouse containing food aid donated by the European Union intended for cyclone victims. The war veterans claimed the project, run by Help, a German NGO, was a front for the MDC.

When a European Union delegation went to the Foreign Ministry to protest, the secretary for foreign affairs, Willard Chiwewe, responded by issuing a statement making further threats. The government, he said, could not guarantee the security of foreign embassies and donor agencies if they became "agents or sympathisers" of political parties.

> Those diplomats who, for whatever reason or background, seek to further the interests of one political party against another, or to act as an agent of one political party against another, may not hope to receive assistance from the ministry. It being understood that, by choosing to side with, or act on behalf of one political party or agent against another, such diplomats would have set aside the relevance and usefulness of this ministry in that regard. It is hereby emphasised that such diplomats would have chosen to meet and live with the fortunes of the party they would have chosen to support.

Chiwewe made similar threats against "overzealous" members and staff of NGOs who indulged in "partisan political work."

Despite a torrent of international protest, the war veteran groups continued to harass foreign aid agencies. Among the targets they chose was Care International, which, with a staff of 120, mostly Zimbabweans, worked on programmes dealing with poverty alleviation, health, nutrition, and emergency relief. Its Canadian director, Dennis O'Brien, was abducted from his Harare office, forced into a pick-up truck, and driven to the Zanu-PF provincial office. When the Canadian High Commissioner, James Wall, attempted to stop the abduction, he was assaulted. The headquarters of an orphans' organisation, SOS Children's Villages, a German-Austrian NGO, which looked after 5,000 orphans, was invaded and temporarily forced to close.

The uproar abroad eventually obliged Mugabe to call off war veteran raids on foreign aid agencies, factories, and offices. The raids in any case had done little to impress the urban population that Mugabe was acting vigorously on their behalf in dealing with recalcitrant employers. But the rest of his campaign against the opposition he pursued as aggressively as before.

MDC officials and supporters, even members of parliament, were constantly harassed and attacked. Party offices were raided. MDC strongholds in Harare, such as Chitungwiza and Mabvuku, were regularly subjected to raids by paramilitary police, soldiers, and the CIO. A Chitungwiza MP, Job Sikhala, was seized at night in his home by soldiers and beaten with rifle butts, chains, and clubs; his pregnant wife was also assaulted. The MP for Mabvuku, Justin Mutendadzamera, and his wife were assaulted in their home by riot police. In broad daylight, a mob of about 200 war veterans and Zanu-PF supporters attacked the home of the MP for Kambuzuma, Willias Madzimure, while he was sitting in parliament, reducing it to a shell. In an attempt to silence Morgan Tsvangirai, state prosecutors charged him under the Law and Order (Maintenance) Act with inciting the violent overthrow of Mugabe's government; the charge related to a speech made by Tsvangirai in September 2000 saying Mugabe should resign or risk being removed violently. Tsvangirai denied the charge, pointing out that, in view of the numerous speeches made by Mugabe and his ministers inciting violence against the opposition and against whites, this was just another example of selective prosecution.

During parliamentary by-elections, the MDC faced a combined onslaught from war veterans, party militias, Zanu-PF youth groups, the police, and the army. The most fiercely contested was a by-election in Bikita West, a rural constituency that the MDC had narrowly won in the general election and that Zanu-PF was determined to wrest back. Directing the campaign were Hunzvi, Chinotimba, and a retired army captain, Francis Zimuto, who liked to be known as "Black Jesus," comparing himself to a "Messiah" liberating the masses from the white man's prison. "Jesus Christ freed humankind from sin," Zimuto explained. "He is the only man who managed to change the life of people the world over. I feel I am like him because I am out to emancipate the people of this country from the world of social oppression. I want to change their life by demanding they be given land."

Zanu-PF militias set up camps around the constituency, beating up people, forcing them to attend rallies, and confiscating identity cards they needed in order to vote. In one village, Hunzvi and his men threw petrol bombs and assaulted four opposition MPs with clubs. Heavily armed police, some of them uniformed war veterans, manned roadblocks used to impede MDC supporters. Addressing a group of villagers in Mureti village, the minister of education, Samuel Mumbengegwi, told them that Zanu-PF would find out from voting registers how people had voted. "We will not be fooled. We will be able to find out who our enemies are and we will ruthlessly deal with them. We want to cleanse this area of all anti-Zanu-PF elements," he said. Chiefs and headmen were warned that they would lose their privileges unless they organised people in their areas to vote for Zanu-PF. Teachers, civil servants, and nurses were told they would be sacked if they supported the MDC. The result was a sizeable victory for Zanu-PF.

Similar tactics were used during a mayoral election in the town of Masvingo. Large numbers of Zanu-PF supporters and war veterans were sent to the town. The police arrested scores of MDC supporters on allegations of public violence, but no Zanu-PF supporters. The provincial governor, Josaya Hungwe, urged supporters "to repeat what you did in Bikita" and declared there would be "total war" if people did not vote for Zanu-PF. "If you do not vote for Zanu-PF in the coming mayoral election, people are going to be killed. I want to tell you that someone is going to die." He rebuked a senior civil servant present in the audience for failing to chant a Zanu-PF slogan when he attended a meeting in the town. All civil servants, he said, were required to chant: "Forward with Zanu-PF and President Mugabe, down with the MDC and Tsvangirai" before conducting any official business with the public. "Zanu-PF is the government which gives you civil servants money and it is led by President Mugabe. We don't tolerate civil servants who address meetings or business functions without making Zanu-PF slogans." Visibly shaken, the senior civil servant stood up and apologised. Just before the election, Zanu-PF forced the entire town to close, ordering all residents to attend a rally addressed by government ministers. These tactics failed to pay off, however; the MDC candidate won the election.

In the courts the MDC pursued its challenge to the previous year's election results in thirty-eight constituencies, arguing that violence, intimidation, fraud, and other irregularities had rendered them invalid. But witnesses willing to testify in the High Court to the violence and intimidation they had suffered swiftly became the target for retribution. The MDC candidate for Kariba, Luka Sigobole, decided to withdraw his petition after he and his family received death threats. "I did it for the safety of our party members," he explained "because people were going to be harassed or even killed."

When three black lawyers travelled to Sadza in the Chikomba constituency to investigate reports that police were assaulting witnesses scheduled to testify in a court case challenging the victory of the Zanu-PF MP, Chenjerai Hunzvi, they quickly ran into difficulty. Arriving in Sadza, they saw a group of about thirty Zanu-PF supporters beating up a witness while uniformed police officers stood by and watched. The assailants turned on the lawyers, calling them "foreigners," "sell-outs," and "stooges of the white man." Two of the lawyers managed to escape, but the third, Tawanda Hondora, chairman of Zimbabwe Lawyers for Human Rights, was caught and severely beaten. Bruised and bleeding, he was marched to the police station, forced to dance and sing Zanu-PF slogans along the way. At the police station he was assaulted by police. When his two colleagues arrived at the police station, they too were detained and assaulted. A police inspector, well known as a war veteran, ordered rifles and live ammunition to be issued and proceeded to lecture the lawyers on the evils of the MDC. They were released after three hours.

The MDC persevered, however, and gained some notable victories. In April Judge James Devittie nullified the results in three constituencies won by Zanu-PF, including Buhera North, where Tsvangirai had stood unsuccessfully, citing massive violence and intimidation. "The law must be obeyed for the well-being of us all and in order that freedom of election may be bequeathed to future generations. I dare not do more than a judge bound by law. Who dares do more is none," said Devittie. After passing judgement Devittie was warned by Chinotimba that he would "soon be following his master"—a reference to the fate of Gubbay. "Devittie is a judge for opposition political parties. The way Gubbay went is the same way Devittie is going to go," said Chinotimba. After receiving death threats, Devittie resigned from the bench.

A sudden sequence of deaths briefly interrupted Mugabe's campaign. In April Border Gezi, a minister responsible for orchestrating much of the violence in Mashonaland Central, was killed in a car crash. In May Moven Mahachi, the defence minister, an old-guard Mugabe loyalist, was also killed in a car crash. Then in June Chenjerai Hunzvi, Mugabe's most fanatical henchman, died in hospital, officially from cerebral malaria but probably from an AIDS-related illness. All three were declared national heroes and buried at Heroes' Acre.

Their deaths shook Zanu-PF to the core. "The party is haunted," said one senior official. "We fear the hand of Lucifer at work." Emmerson Mnangagwa remarked: "We don't know what is hitting us. Something unnatural must be behind this." Some officials interpreted the deaths as a sign that the party should relent on its campaign of violence and terror.

But Mugabe, although shaken, was determined to press on. "Fate has been most unkind to us, hitting us where it hurts most at a time when our land-based Third Chimurenga is at its most critical historical juncture," he said at Hunzvi's funeral. "And yet these harsh reversals should never deter us, but should, instead, propel us to fight even harder to intensify the campaign and ensure that the sacrifices of our fallen heroes are not in vain." Describing Hunzvi as a champion of social justice, Mugabe declared: "There can be no greater tribute and honour paid him than that which ensures that the fast-track land resettlement programme is intensified. We must see the campaign through to its glorious finish."

Later that month Mugabe duly announced the expropriation of a further 2,000 white-owned farms, bringing the total number to about 5,000 farms, covering 19 million acres. This meant that about 95 percent of the members of the Commercial Farmers Union were now affected by expropriation orders. Mugabe accompanied his announcement with another tirade against white farmers, accusing them of "hostile acts" against the government. Explaining the government's land policy to a group of church leaders, who sat shaking their heads in disbelief, the justice minister, Patrick Chinamasa, declared: "Violence is a necessary tool for a successful land reform programme."

An upsurge of violent incidents hit the white farming community. Squatters and war veterans laid siege to farming families in their homes, destroyed crops and seed beds, wrecked farm equipment, cut off water supplies, and set fire to grazing land. An elderly white farmer died after being struck on the head with an axe.

The worst outbreak of violence occurred in August in the Chinhoyi farming district, sixty miles northwest of Harare. It started after a group of government ministers and MPs, including Ignatius Chombo, Mugabe's local government minister, Phillip Chiyangwa, the millionaire businessman recently elected as MP for Chinhoyi, and Sabina Mugabe, Mugabe's sister, visited a Chinhoyi farm urging invaders there to take over neighbouring farms. The following day, a mob of some fifty war veterans and invaders laid siege to the homestead on Liston Shiels Farm. Responding to a distress call over the local radio network from the farmer, Anthony Barkley, a convoy of white farmers forced their way through the mob. In the mêlée, five invaders and two farmers were seriously injured. The police eventually arrived and requested the white farmers to report to Chinhoyi police station to give statements. When they arrived at the police station they were arrested, charged with inciting "public violence." When the elderly father of one of the arrested men arrived at the police station to deliver a blanket for his son, he too was arrested. Five other whites who went to the police station to check on the welfare of their colleagues were also arrested and charged.

The incident was seized on by the government to claim that white farmers had deliberately provoked the violence. "It's true the farmers have been attacking people," the minister of home affairs, John Nkomo, said on state television. "It's the farmers who have been unleashing this violence." On the streets of Chinhoyi, Zanu-PF supporters retaliated against whites at random, assaulting shoppers and stoning cars. At the magistrate's court a hostile crowd gathered, shouting abuse when twenty-one white farmers appeared for a bail hearing. They were held in prison for two weeks, their heads forcibly shaved, before bail was granted.

Across the Chinhoyi district, Zanu-PF mobs went on the rampage, burning down and looting farmhouses; stealing tractors, vehicles, equipment, and fertiliser; slaughtering cattle and driving off entire herds of livestock. Police officers participated in the raids, using police vehicles to ferry groups of attackers to farms and to take away loot. Scores of white families fled the area, abandoning their homes.

On Two Treehill Farm, twenty miles north of Chinhoyi, the Geldenhuys family were woken up in the early morning by a mob of about seventy Zanu-PF supporters who arrived in stolen vehicles and began loading up fertiliser, seed, and equipment. When Charl Geldenhuys confronted them, they shot his dog and then opened fire on him, missing narrowly. He retreated to the homestead, remaining besieged there with his wife, young daughter, and six-month-old infant for nine hours. In mid-afternoon a team of Zanu-PF politicians arrived—Chombo, Chiyangwa, and Peter Chanetsa, the provincial governor—accompanied by a police escort. While a state television crew filmed the proceedings, they began to interrogate the Geldenhuys couple, claiming they had provoked the violence. Chiyangwa pointed menacingly at Charl Geldenhuys, accusing him of shooting his own dog. The couple painstakingly denied doing so. Clutching her infant, Tertia Geldenhuys pleaded with Chombo, "Minister, we are God-fearing people." Chombo told them to pack their belongings and leave. They left that night.

In a subsequent incident in the same area, Chiyangwa was unwittingly filmed by a television crew giving instructions in chiShona to a group of Zanu-PF youths. "If you get hold of MDC supporters, beat them until they are dead. Burn their farms and their workers' houses, then run away fast and we will blame the burning of the workers' houses on the whites. Report to the police, because they are ours."

The violence spread to other areas, to Mhangura and Doma in the north, then to Hwedza in the east. As well as white farmers, thousands of farm labourers and their families were forced to abandon their homes, taking with them what meagre possessions they could carry, camping by the roadside. Many had been born on the farms and had no other homes to go to. They headed for nearby towns, hoping to find shelter.

Mugabe's victims also included black commercial farmers who supported the MDC. The most prominent was Philemon Matibe, a successful Chegutu farmer who had stood in the 2000 parliamentary elections and who had then challenged the result when he lost. He was told that if he dropped his election petition he would be allowed to continue farming, but he refused. Shortly afterwards a mob, eighty strong, led by the local district administrator and four policemen, arrived on his 1,100-acre farm in a convoy of vehicles. The district administrator ordered the Matibe family to leave forthwith and immediately handed out plots to Zanu-PF supporters, including a banker and three police officers. Matibe lost everything: his home, his livelihood, his life savings that he had poured into the farm. "This is not about correcting a colonial imbalance," he said. "This is about punishing your enemies and rewarding your friends. This is about staying in power no matter what the damage is to your country or its democracy."

With so many farms disrupted, destroyed, and left untended, Zimbabwe now faced serious food shortages to add to its list of woes. Public protests against the plague of lawlessness and disorder afflicting Zimbabwe became ever louder. At a meeting of its twenty member churches, the Zimbabwe Council of Churches, usually a docile organisation, accused Mugabe of plunging the country into "a de facto state of warfare" in his bid to stay in power:

> Land reform, universally agreed upon as a matter of utmost urgency, has been twisted into a fast-track to further the self-aggrandisement of the chefs and misery for the masses. What should have improved the lot of every Zimbabwean is now viewed as irrevocably partisan, and is associated with disorder, violence and displacement.

The economy, the churches continued, was "in tatters"; unemployment had soared; health and education services had deteriorated:

> Collectively, all of this has left the average Zimbabwean on the verge of utter destitution and hopelessness. All of this points to a very obvious deficiency in the leadership and governance of our country. Those who have been entrusted with authority have abused it. The various arms of the state have become rotten with corruption, nepotism and self-interest. The law has become a farce, used only to further the interests of a selected few.

Fearing that Zimbabwe's descent into chaos would damage the entire southern African region, the leaders of neighbouring African states—South Africa, Mozambique, Botswana, Malawi, and Zambia —sought to intervene. "The situation has become untenable when it is seen that the highest office in that land seems to support illegal means of land reform, land invasions... beating up of people, blood flowing everywhere," said a prominent South African official, Tito Mboweni. "I am saying this as forcefully as I am because the developments in Zimbabwe are affecting us and are stressing us unnecessarily....The wheels have come off there." At a summit meeting in Harare in September 2001, African leaders from southern Africa remonstrated with Mugabe, trying to get him to change direction, but to no avail.

A Commonwealth initiative was launched in an attempt to persuade Mugabe to restore law and order in exchange for international funds to assist a properly planned land reform programme. The plan was similar to the 1998 land agreement that Mugabe had signed but then ignored. Once again Mugabe accepted the terms of the deal—known as the Abuja agreement—but land occupations and lawlessness continued unabated.

In November 2001 Mugabe delivered his final blow. By presidential decree, he ordered the expropriation of virtually all white-owned farms without compensation. Farmers were told they would be given ninety days to vacate their homes and properties and threatened with imprisonment if they tried to interfere.

Among members of Mugabe's cabinet, there were growing misgivings about the headlong plunge he had taken. But Mugabe dismissed them as "doubting Thomases." After one minister resigned, fleeing the country, he retorted: "I do not want ministers who are in the habit of running away. I want those I can call *amadoda sibili* [real men], people with spine....Our revolution...was not fought by cowards. If some of you are getting weak-kneed, tell us and we will continue the struggle."

# [14]

# ENDGAME

IN A RADIO BROADCAST from Mozambique in 1976 during the Rhodesian war, Mugabe summed up his view of electoral democracy:

> Our votes must go together with our guns. After all, any vote we shall have, shall have been the product of the gun. The gun which produces the vote should remain its security officer—its guarantor. The people's votes and the people's guns are always inseparable twins.

Mugabe has held fast to this creed. Whatever challenge his regime has faced, he has always been prepared to overcome it by resorting to the gun. So proud was he of his record that in 2000 he boasted about having "a degree in violence." His ministers followed suit. "The area of violence is an area where Zanu-PF has a very strong, long and successful history," Nathan Shamuyarira, one of Mugabe's closest colleagues, declared.

What propelled Mugabe to use violence so readily was his obsession with power. Power for Mugabe was not a means to an end, but the end itself. His overriding ambition, he once admitted, was to achieve total control, and he pursued that objective with relentless single-mindedness, crushing opponents and critics who stood in his way.

Mugabe's single-mindedness was evident from an early age. Making few friends, he devoted his time to studying, encouraged by Jesuit teachers who recognised his intellectual ability and his aptitude for self-discipline. His Jesuit upbringing instilled in him a self-belief that he never lost. But teaching rather than politics seemed to be his destiny.

The colonial regime under which Mugabe grew up, however, engendered in him an abiding sense of bitterness. Rhodesia's whites were generally contemptuous of the African population, treating them as an inferior race, demanding unfailing obedience to white rule. "We feared the white man," Mugabe recalled. "He was power. He had guns." Fear and distrust of white society were part of everyday life, deeply ingrained.

The contrast that Mugabe found in Ghana when he arrived there on a teaching contract in 1958 was striking. In its first years of independence, Ghana was widely admired as a beacon of hope in Africa, bursting with plans for a new socialist order and keen to support the liberation of the rest of Africa from European rule. It was in this heady atmosphere that Mugabe became a convert to Marxist ideas and saw the prospect of a different future for Rhodesia. His commitment to teaching nevertheless remained firm.

Only by chance, during what was supposed to be a brief return visit to Rhodesia in 1960, did Mugabe abruptly change course. Caught up unexpectedly in the turmoil of African protest against white rule, he threw himself into the nationalist cause with the same dedication he had hitherto devoted to teaching. He was among the first nationalists to advocate armed struggle, convinced that nothing else would overcome white intransigence.

Eleven years of imprisonment hardened his resolve. Whereas Nelson Mandela used his prison years to open a dialogue with South Africa's white rulers, Mugabe emerged from prison adamantly opposed to any idea of negotiation, as he made clear to African presidents at the Lusaka summit in 1974. His aim by then was to overthrow white society by force and to replace it with a one-party Marxist regime. In 1979, after seven years of civil war in which at least 30,000 people had died, when a negotiated settlement was within reach at Lancaster House in London, Mugabe still hankered for military victory, "the ultimate joy."

That he was denied the chance of a military victory was always something of a disappointment to him. Although the Lancaster House deal opened the way to his election as head of Zimbabwe's new government, he still aspired to the kind of power that military victory would have given him. The advent of democracy for Mugabe was not the final goal but a stepping stone towards achieving greater control through the establishment of a one-party state.

To that end, he unleashed a campaign of mass murder and brutality on the Ndebele and Kalanga people, determined to destroy their support for his main rival, Zapu.

The one-party system that Mugabe developed, following the demise of Zapu in 1987, lasted for twelve years. He accumulated huge personal power, ensuring that Zanu-PF's grip extended into every corner of the government's apparatus. One by one, the state media, parastatal organisations, the police, the civil service and, eventually, the courts, were subordinated to Mugabe's will, giving him control of a vast system of patronage.

Whatever good intentions he started out with—plans for improved education and health facilities—soon diminished in importance. For all his talk of striving for socialism, Mugabe never displayed much concern for the welfare of common people. The main beneficiaries of independence, all too clearly, were Zanu-PF's ruling elite, who engaged in a relentless scramble for jobs, contracts, farms, and businesses that Mugabe was content to condone as a means of fortifying his own power base. Under his one-party system, the scramble became ever more frenetic, spawning corruption on a massive scale.

His self-belief grew into a monstrous ego. Surrounded by syco-
phants, he knew few restraints. Only his first wife, Sally, managed to
exert a calming influence on his ambition and anger. After her death
in 1992 he became increasingly detached from reality. His destiny,
he believed, was to rule for as long as he wanted.

The shock of his defeat in the referendum in 2000 was thus all
the more profound. His reaction was to resort to the methods that
had served him so well in the past: violence and intimidation. White
farmers became his most immediate target, subjected to months of
terror tactics. In a bid to whip up popular support, he also unleashed a torrent of racist abuse against the entire white community, displaying an innate fear and loathing of whites in general.
Although most blacks ignored such incitement, Mugabe's followers
took their cue from it, confident that acting in a hostile and aggressive manner towards white victims was part of official policy.

Mugabe's ultimate objective, however, was to destroy all opposition to his regime. Determined to remain in power, he used all the
resources of the government to attack his opponents, sanctioning
murder, torture, and lawlessness of every kind. "No matter what
force you have, this is my territory and that which is mine I cling
[to] unto death," he said in 2001.

The cost of this strategy has been enormous. Zimbabwe has
been reduced to a bankrupt and impoverished state, threatened by
economic collapse and catastrophic food shortages. Opposition
leaders railed against such a ruinous course. Morgan Tsvangirai described Mugabe as "a deranged despot"; Edgar Tekere called him
"an insane head of state."

But there was a crude logic to Mugabe's actions. His sole purpose had become to hold on to power. Whatever the cost, his
regime was dedicated towards that end. Violence had paid off in the
past; he expected it to secure the future.

# SELECT BIBLIOGRAPHY

Alexander, Jocelyn. "Dissident Perspectives in Zimbabwe's Post-Independence War." *Africa* 68 no. 2 (1998): pp 151–182.

Alexander, Jocelyn, JoAnn McGregor, and Terence Ranger. *Violence and Memory; One Hundred Years in the "Dark Forests" of Matabeleland.* Oxford: Currey, 2000.

Astrow, Andre. *Zimbabwe: A Revolution That Lost Its Way.* London: Zed Press, 1983.

Auret, Diana. *Reaching for Justice: The Catholic Commission for Justice and Peace, 1972–1992.* Gweru, Zimbabwe: Mambo Press, 1992.

Bhebe, Ngwabi, and Terence Ranger, eds. *Society in Zimbabwe's Liberation War.* London: Currey, 1995.

———. *Soldiers in Zimbabwe's Liberation War.* London: Currey, 1995.

Buckle, Catherine. *African Tears: The Zimbabwe Land Invasions.* Johannesburg, South Africa: Covos Day, 2001.

Catholic Commission for Justice and Peace, Legal Resources Foundation. *Breaking the Silence, Building True Peace: A Report on the Disturbances in Matabeleland and the Midlands, 1980 to 1988.* Harare, Zimbabwe: CCJP/LRF, 1997.

Caute, David. *Under the Skin: The Death of White Rhodesia.* London: Penguin, 1983.

Charlton, Michael. *The Last Colony in Africa: Diplomacy and the Independence of Rhodesia.* Oxford: Blackwell, 1990.

de Waal, Victor. *The Politics of Reconciliation: Zimbabwe's First Decade.* London: Hurst, 1990.

Flower, Ken. *Serving Secretly: An Intelligence Chief on Record, Rhodesia into Zimbabwe, 1964–1981*. London: Murray, 1987.

Godwin, Peter. *Mukiwa: A White Boy in Africa*. London: Macmillan, 1996.

Godwin, Peter, and Ian Hancock. *Rhodesians Never Die: The Impact of War and Political Change on White Rhodesia, c1970–1980*. London: Oxford University Press, 1993.

Herbst, Jeffrey. *State Politics in Zimbabwe*. Berkeley: University of California Press, 1990.

Kriger, Norma J. "The Politics of Creating National Heroes: The Search for Political Legitimacy and National Identity." In Ngwabi Bhebe and Terence Ranger, eds., *Soldiers in Zimbabwe's Liberation War*. London: Currey, 1995.

———. *Zimbabwe's Guerrilla War: Peasant Voices*. Oxford: Cambridge University Press, 1992.

Lawyers Committee for Human Rights. *Zimbabwe: Wages of War*. New York: LCHR, 1986.

Lessing, Doris. *African Laughter*. London: HarperCollins, 1982.

Lelyveld, Joseph. *Move Your Shadow: South Africa Black and White*. London: Joseph, 1986.

Linden, Ian. *The Catholic Church and the Struggle for Zimbabwe*. London: Longman, 1980.

Makumbe, John, and Daniel Compagnon. *Behind the Smokescreen: The Politics of Zimbabwe's 1995 General Elections*. Harare: University of Zimbabwe, 2000.

Mandaza, Ibbo, ed. *Zimbabwe: The Political Economy of Transition, 1980–86*. Dakar, Senegal: Codesria, 1986.

Mandaza, Ibbo, and Lloyd M. Sachikonye, eds. *The One-Party State and Democracy: The Zimbabwe Debate*. Harare, Zimbabwe: Sapes Trust, 1991.

Martin, David, and Phyllis Johnson. *The Struggle for Zimbabwe*. London: Faber, 1981.

McLaughlin, Janice. *On the Frontline: Catholic Missions in Zimbabwe's Liberation War*. Harare, Zimbabwe: Baobab Books, 1996.

Meredith, Martin. *The Past Is Another Country: Rhodesia, UDI to Zimbabwe*. London: Pan, 1980.

Moyo, Jonathan N. *Voting for Democracy: A Study of Electoral Politics in Zimbabwe*. Harare: University of Zimbabwe, 1992.

Mugabe, Robert. *Our War of Liberation: Speeches, Articles, Interviews,* 1976–1979. Gweru, Zimbabwe: Mambo Press, 1983.

Mutasa, Didymus. *Black Behind Bars: Rhodesia,* 1959–1974. Harare, Zimbabwe: Longman, 1983.

Ncube, Welshman. "Constitutionalism, Democracy and Political Practice in Zimbabwe." In Ibbo Mandaza and Lloyd M. Sachikonye, eds., *The One-Party State and Democracy.* Harare, Zimbabwe: Sapes Trust, 1991.

Nkomo, Joshua. *The Story of My Life.* London: Methuen, 1984.

Nyagumbo, Maurice. *With the People.* Salisbury, Rhodesia: Graham Publishing, 1980.

Palmer, Robin. *Land & Racial Discrimination in Rhodesia.* London: Heinemann, 1977.

Ranger, Terence. *Peasant Consciousness and Guerrilla War in Zimbabwe.* London: Currey, 1985.

Shamuyarira, Nathan. *Crisis in Rhodesia.* London: Deutsch, 1965.

Sithole, Masipula. *Zimbabwe: Struggles Within the Struggle,* 1957–1980. Harare, Zimbabwe: Rujeko, 1999.

Smith, David, and Simpson Colin. *Mugabe.* London: Sphere, 1981.

Smith, Ian. *The Great Betrayal.* London: Blake, 1997.

Stiff, Peter. *Cry Zimbabwe: Independence — Twenty Years On.* Johannesburg, South Africa: Galago, 2000.

Stoneman, Colin. *Zimbabwe's Prospects: Issues of Race, Class, State and Capital in Southern Africa.* London: Macmillan, 1988.

Stoneman, Colin, and Lionel Cliffe. *Zimbabwe: Politics, Economics and Society.* London: Pinter, 1990.

Vambe, Lawrence. *From Rhodesia to Zimbabwe.* London: Heinemann, 1976.

———. *An Ill-Fated People: Zimbabwe before and after Rhodes.* London: Heinemann, 1972.

Verrier, Anthony. *The Road to Zimbabwe,* 1890–1980. London: Cape, 1986.

Werbner, Richard P. "In Memory: A Heritage of War in Southwestern Zimbabwe." In Ngwabi Bhebe and Terence Ranger, eds., *Society in Zimbabwe's Liberation War.* London: Currey, 1995.

———. *Tears of the Dead.* Edinburgh: Edinburgh University Press, 1991.

Zimbabwe Human Rights Association. *Choosing the Path to Peace and Development: Coming to Terms with Human Rights Violations of the 1982–87 Conflict in Matabeleland and Midlands Province.* Harare, Zimbabwe: ZHRA, 1999.

# INDEX